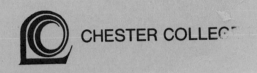

GODFREY ASHBY

SACRIFICE

Its Nature and Purpose

SCM PRESS LTD

British Library Cataloguing in Publication Data

Ashby, G. W. E. C. (Godfrey W. E. C.)
Sacrifice.
1. Christian doctrine. Sacrifice
I. Title
234

ISBN 0–334–01437–9

First published 1988
by SCM Press Ltd
26–30 Tottenham Road, London N1

Typeset by The Spartan Press Ltd
Lymington, Hants
and printed in Great Britain by
Richard Clay Ltd
Bungay, Suffolk

To My Family,
St John's College, Cambridge,
and the Diocese of St John's, Transkei

CONTENTS

One   Introduction   1

Two   The Coinage of Sacrifice   5

Three   Sacrifice in the Hebrew Tradition   26

Four   Christian Sacrifice   49

Five   The Passover – the Missing Link   69

Six   Sacrifice and the Eucharist   102

Seven   Filling up the Sacrifice   123

Bibliography   137

Index of Names   146

Index of References   150

ONE

INTRODUCTION

'Sacrifice is a language used by all, but understood by none' (Hicks 1946: 3, quoting Glover). This remark is a challenge, provoking two possible responses: first that sacrifice is a language in the widest sense of communication; secondly that nobody has understood sacrifice. We hope to engage in both these areas, the negative and the positive, in this work.

Sacrifice is basic to biblical language, to biblical religion. It is also basic to most non-biblical religions of the world. The actual practices of sacrifice and their elements   the 'victims', the offerers, the priesthood, the deities and spirits, are still enacted in many cultures and religions and are described at length in their Hebrew forms in the Old Testament. The larger portion of mankind has firsthand experience of the act of sacrifice. The language of sacrifice, whether used literally or metaphorically, occurs frequently and in crucial places in the New Testament and in much modern speech. This work is devoted to the study of sacrifice. Its purpose is to free sacrifice of the many misunderstandings that are current about it, to understand and appreciate it, to explore all the available evidence from various disciplines and to open up and mine a rich vein of faith through this ancient custom embedded in human intuition by some archetypal conscience.

Sacrifice involves the material and the physical – people, animals and things, life as it is lived. Sacrifice also involves drama and liturgy, whether exceedingly simple or excessively complicated. It is theatre. Sacrifice involves the unseen world of the Spirit or of the spirits. It involves a conscious or unconscious leap of faith. Because of what it involves, sacrifice raises many problems for many people, particularly for Westerners and even for religious Westerners (perhaps more so for them). For those who feel that matter, the stuff of this world, is too gross or seductive for the world of the Spirit, the use of bodies, of feasts, of animals or vegetables or even of wine and water, in order to communicate with a God who is to be worshipped in Spirit, is abhorrent. For those who find the world of the Spirit irrelevant to the material world and see it as Frederick the Great did, as an 'opiate for the people', sacrifice, which by its very nature involves the unseen, is abhorrent, and means pandering to a chimera. For those who are revolted by all bloodshedding and consider it to be primitive, crude and totally unnecessary, no matter what its purpose, sacrifice is abhorrent. For those who have a rooted instinct of aversion to any theatre or (within Christianity) to any representation of the death of Christ as being in any way reputable, sacrifice is abhorrent. For those who see mature religious beliefs and practices as being primarily concerned with ethics and right behaviour, sacrifice is an irrelevance and, as a distraction, abhorrent. If the main aim of religion is to prevent the butler from stealing the silver, then sacrifice can be of little use. There has been much anti-sacrificial theology in the Western world. This has born fruit in the following popular opinions about sacrifice. These do not need authors or works, since they are so common. Needless to say that they are not the opinions of many serious scholars of the subject.

1. 'Sacrifice' has come to be used in the English language (and in other European languages) as a synonym for 'giving up' – often the giving up of something relatively trivial, such as the giving up of sweets for the days of Lent. No mention is usually made of the recipient of the sacrifice: no liturgy is usually involved. The word has lost its real meaning and become 'ill-sorted'.

2. Sacrifice has been 'spiritualized' or moralized, so that it deals with intangibles, such as praises, good deeds and the like. Here again, no liturgy is usually involved, or else, as in the case of the Anglican prayer book, one instinctively feels that this meaning is given to sacrifice to exclude something else (i.e. a reference to Christ's actual sacrifice). This represents a very old tendency in the Christian church, as will be seen below. Its antiquity does not totally excuse its emasculation of the meaning of the word.

3. Sacrifice has been identified with *human* sacrifice, and caused widespread revulsion against sacrifice as a whole. This has been encouraged by popular fiction and by stories of missionaries in

cooking pots. Human sacrifice is in fact not to be identified with cannibalism, is a comparatively rare practice and has always been so, globally considered, within recorded time.

4. Sacrifice has a grim connotation, being linked with death, blood, cruelty, loss and suffering.

5. Sacrifice has been slanted by the Christian eucharistic debate, which has been allowed to backfire into the meaning and purpose of sacrifice. Those who see the eucharist as a fellowship meal only have tended to see sacrifice as primarily a community feast, while those who see the eucharist as sacrifice have tended to see sacrifice in terms of propitiation or expiation. 'Comparative religion has inherited an ancient sectarian quarrel about the value of formal ritual' (Douglas 1966: 62), since added to the theological debate about the eucharist is the debate about the use of ceremonial. This is a clear instance of academic partiality.

6. Sacrifice has been described as a pagan practice, a primitive, unenlightened habit inherited and superseded by Christians from Hebraism which in turn took it over from Canaanite and other Middle Eastern peoples (Koehler 1957: 181ff.) This is an old tendency going back to a general unease about anything that did not have narrowly and specifically Christian origins and a specific unease about anything shared with Judaism.

7. Co-operation between anthropologists and theologians and the sharing of common insights has not always been notable, though the mutual openness of the two disciplines has been growing. There have been theologians and biblical scholars who have settled for some school of anthropology that suited their assumptions. Hence Frazer's *Golden Bough* has had a predominance in theological circles long after it had ceased to be the definitive work for anthropologists. Similarly there have been anthropologists who have advanced theories about the biblical material without any reference to any biblical studies since the Authorized Version of the Bible.

As we shall see, much work has been done in recent years to rehabilitate sacrifice. The following factors have contributed to the recovery of interest in what is perhaps the most basic and widespread phenomenon in religious experience:

(i) Religious thinking is no longer completely dominated by Western theology, even in the realm of Christian theology alone. The last decade has seen a rapid expansion of theological writing from Africa, Asia and Latin America. In many of these ancient cultures, sacrifice is still an established practice and is alive and well. Even if Christ's sacrifice is accepted as fulfilling all sacrifice, the insights about what sacrifice means come fresh from a culture that knows what sacrifice means by experience.

(ii) The tendencies in Western theology that saw all issues in terms of moral imperatives no longer dominate. In Old Testament theology for example, the prophets are no longer seen as the great moralizers who transformed a ritualistic, legalistic Semitic religion into a lofty moral code. There is more interest in and sympathy for ritual practice such as sacrifice.

(iii) Various approaches in Old Testament Studies and in anthropology such as the growth-of-tradition approach and the structuralist approach among others call for a re-examination of sacrifice.

(iv) For Christians there will always arise the question – if so much is made in the New Testament of Christ's *sacrifice* on the Cross, then the practice of sacrifice must surely be basic to any understanding of what he did? A whole chapter will be devoted to this.

(v) Finally there is the riddle of continuity. In most societies where sacrifice is practiced, it takes the form of a repeated event. What happens to it when the claim is made that one sacrifice has been offered once and for all and that no further victims need be offered? How is that one sacrifice translated into the continuing life of the community – by sacrament, by moral obedience, by suffering, by proclamation? What happens when the practice of sacrifice has fallen into desuetude?

The assumption that is made here is that sacrifice and what it means is germane to religions, integral to those religions which draw their inspiration from all or part of the Bible, and vital to Christianity.

TWO

THE COINAGE OF SACRIFICE

The practice of sacrifice is basic to most religions. It is worldwide and occurs in areas and among people separated by geography for such long periods and by such vast distances as to make conscious imitation or collusion on a global scale remote indeed. Durkheim, examining sacrificial rites practised in Central Australia, described them as containing 'all the essential principles of a great religious institution which was destined to become one of the foundation stones of the positive cult in the superior religions: this is the institution of sacrifice' (1961: 377, 388). This is an interesting comment from Durkheim, and the phrase 'was destined to become' raises the question of whether religious customs such as sacrifice are destined to become foundational by virtue of conscious or unconscious widespread adoption by societies, or because the urge to sacrifice is borne into societies by an archetypal will. There can be very few peoples who have never sacrificed in the course of history. Even where no 'primitive' physical rite of sacrifice has survived, the terminology or sacrifice has passed into the theological language and has become embedded in the basic creeds of what Durkheim would call 'the superior religions'. This is particularly true of Islam, Judaism and Christianity. Their sacred writings abound in references to literal sacrifices and even more with the language of sacrifice. The language of sacrifice is integral to the language of religion.

It is very difficult to define what sacrifice is. In most languages there are words, old words, which can be loosely translated by the English word 'sacrifice' but these words in fact described certain acts of sacrifice or certain types of sacrifice, but in themselves give little clue as the basic meaning of the action. This is to be seen in the vocabulary of the two biblical languages, Greek and Hebrew. It seems that to identify a sacrifice was easy, whereas to attempt the philosophy behind it was difficult and not often attempted. Perhaps this is asking too much in any case. Most people know what it is to think, whereas few would venture into the epistemology or psychology of thought.

Perhaps the Latin word *sacrificium* was the first attempt to give some explanation of the action of sacrificing rather than merely identifying it. '*Sacer*' means 'holy' and '*facere*' means 'to make'. Quite how the Romans came to use this word for the acts they performed in their cultus is unknown. Nevertheless they succeeded in producing a word that has added further confusion to an already difficult problem. Feeding back into contemporary language the roots of words is a risky pastime, however interesting. For example, 'Elephant and Castle' may well be a corruption of 'Infanta da Castile', but it is no help in identifying the location of a district in South London today. Sacrifice is not merely 'making holy' since this says either too little or too much. There are many ways of making holy which are not sacrifices and many sacrifices which to all intents do not make holy. Those words which appears to define the meaning of sacrifice, such as 'suffering, sacrament and sacrifice' are useful umbrella terms but not explanations of why people have sacrificed and do sacrifice. Also, many attempts have been made to define the sacrifices of one set of people at one particular historical period in terms of the understandings of a later period. This is the way of anachronism. For example, even if it could be proved that in Old Israel, sacrifices were always communion meals, this does not prove that Christians of the first century AD understood sacrifices as a communion meal. Similarly if Protestant Christians can only accept sacrifice as a communion meal, this does not prove that Old Israel understood all its sacrifices as communion meals. Such explanations and classifications leave a trail of *non sequiturs*. All sorts of criteria of 'morality', ritual and magic have been applied as value judgments and made to fit all cases. Two examples of Procrustean definitions of sacrifice will suffice.

1. Jastrow (quoted in Yerkes 1953: 156) noticed that some Near Eastern sacrificial rites included hepatoscopy: from this he deduced that the whole practice of animal sacrifice arose out of a surgical need – to get at the liver and inspect it. Animal sacrifice is merely a way of liver extraction. Presumably sacrifices that involved no hepatoscopic ritual were instances where the liver had been forgotten! Such a definition is at least unsubtle. Many other definitions are much more subtle and question-begging.

2. 'Sacrifice means direct surrender to God without any thought of social usefulness. The sacrificial animal is killed and burnt for the god; the wine of sacrifice is poured out for him. All life belongs to God and is to be consecrated to Him, directly, to Him, personally, to Himself. The most important sacrifice is that which is intended to remove some obstacle which has come in between God and man: the atoning or expiatory sacrifice' (Brunner 1934: 476). What has happened here is just one example (to be fair to Brunner) of the imposing of one brand of Christian theology upon the universal practice of sacrifice. The agenda is clear – the surrender to the absolute and all-demanding God must come first – elements of social usefulness must be removed for fear of Pelagianism, the action must be made direct (excluding priestly intermediaries) and the removal of sin in terms of obstacles between God and man must be the prime purpose. Thus, with this agenda a definition of sacrifice is reached, whether this fits all sacrifices or not.

Sacrifice in fact poses problems which no verbal derivations or anachronistic theological or anthropological categories will solve. The impulse to sacrifice is so basic to mankind that in Christ it became the basis of the event that Christians have seen as the most important event in the world's history. What can be said about sacrifice that holds good for all sacrifices? What can be said that holds good for sacrifice in the Judaeo-Christian tradition in particular?

First, sacrifice involves action, drama, ritual, worship, however rudimentary or sophisticated. It is not merely a technique, though from time to time those who perform it may see it as a technique. It is always understood as being effective, as *doing something*. It is difficult to avoid the word 'magic' in this connection, because magic and ritual overlap. A ritual is performed because it is supposed to effect something, to bring about some change or other. Magic is also supposed to be effective. Unfortunately magic is often further defined as a device for manipulating the supernatural powers whether they are willing to listen or not and thereby obtains a pejorative sense. We would do well to avoid the word magic even though it need not have this sense. There are problems enough with words germane to sacrifice without creating further ones.

So sacrifice 'does something'. Further, it is creative, creating what Mary Douglas (1966: 72) called 'harmonious worlds'. In the 'doing' of sacrifice there are actors in the drama. Someone has to give the sacrifice and he, or someone acting for him, must officiate at the rite. Someone slays the animal if it is an animal sacrifice. Someone *unseen* receives the sacrifice (or, occasionally, rejects it). There are dramatis personae, even if the cast be reduced to a giver and a receiver. There is a way of doing it, however simple. There is a rite, a set form. For example, the sacrificial rites of the Nuer and Lo-Dagaa peoples of Sudan have been carefully studied (Evans-Pritchard 1956, Goody 1962). The personnel involved are minimal but the rites surprisingly fixed and most certainly living and meaningful. Special places are used. There is implied in these rites, as in all sacrifices, belief in the reality of what is being done – that real people are doing the offering, that real beings are receiving the offering and that what is being done is real. Once this faith ceases or is denied, then the act becomes lifeless and will eventually fall away, though it may be cynically kept up for a while for the sake of the community or out of regard for tradition. It is essential to remember that in dealing with sacrifice we are not dealing with a mechanical economic transaction but with an act which expresses the faith that a relationship is possible between the offerer and the unseen receiver of the sacrifice. Hence Beattie remarks (1964: 234), 'We can only understand it if we ask not only what the people who practise it are trying to do, but also what they are trying to say and in what language they are trying to say it.'

Secondly, in the action of sacrifice, some change occurs in the object that is sacrificed. It is perhaps best to avoid the technical term, 'victim', since this has acquired emotive overtones which are usually absent from sacrifices. This change involves, in the case of human or animal sacrifice, death, which accounts for the grim macabre reputation of sacrificial rites. It is essential to appreciate that, even in human sacrifice, the death of the living creature is not seen as a tragedy, any more than the death of a sheep is today seen as a tragedy before roast mutton. Human sacrifice is of course an unusual case: even there many circumstances have to be considered. Yet sacrifice is not primarily a death rite. It would be nearer the truth to say that death is incidental. Immolation usually takes place within the rite itself, but it is not the essence of the rite. All sacrificial theories that concentrate on killing or on death are at best partial explanations.

Whatever might have originally been the psychological reason for sacrificing, it is very unlikely that Money-Kyrle is right in positing an unconscious desire to kill the 'Old Man' or father-figure as the rationale for sacrificing (1930). We would then be left with innumerable occasions of sacrifice when we would have to invent an old man, a wraith from forgotten past. Money-Kyrle's theories rested on unconscious motives derived from those of Freud. The latter's well-known example (1955: 141–2) ran thus: 'One day the brothers who had been driven out [of the horde by its jealous leader] came together, killed and devoured their father and so made an end of the patriarchal horde . . . . The totem meal, which is perhaps man's earliest festival, would thus be a repetition and a commemoration of this memorable and criminal deed, which was the beginning of so many things, of social organization, of moral restrictions and of religion.' To this Money-Kyrle added the comment: 'It is no great flight of fancy to see in the sacrifice of a god more than a mere parallel to the slaughter of a father' (1930: 188). It is amazing that, whereas Kipling's *Just-so Stories* are accepted as delightful pseudo-aetiologies and enjoyed for their entertainment value, the imposition of a structural just-so story (which might conceivably fit a certain number of examples if we could ever be sure that our evidence is accurate) upon a universal practise such as sacrifice, has been taken so seriously by scholars, theologians and anthropologists alike. It is always possible to ignore the historical situations and contemporary explanations of any ritual practice, including sacrifice. Indeed the structuralist approach would seem to be a desperate solution where evidence as to why sacrifice is done is so conflicting. Is there in fact much difference between imposing a theological archetype on sacrifice (i.e. 'God has commanded it, no matter how it is actually understood'), and imposing a linguistic archetype (a certain juxtaposition of themes, e.g. binary opposites etc., will work out a certain purpose in the society where they occur, irrespective of the idiom, or the time, or the place, or the participants, or the historical period)? Are we much further advanced in our understanding of sacrifice if we claim that it is a society's way of dealing with a liminal situation? We still then have to define liminal situations, explain what lies to either side of the liminal and explain why sacrifice has to be the solution. So also with the incest motif. This motif may well connect up with the behaviour of some human offerers or even with the legendary behaviour of some of the members of the pantheon, where there is thought to be one. Nevertheless as an explanation of sacrifice as a whole it smells very strongly of a Viennese lamp.

In point of fact, many acts of sacrifice do not involve the killing of an animal. This is true of many West African sacrifices. It is of course possible to claim that these are all substitutionary but proof of this assertion as a general theory would be lacking. The burning or eating of cereals, the pouring out of libations of water, oil, milk or wine are regarded as sacrifices by those who practise them. Naturally it is possible to claim that they imply a 'little death' of the product involved – destruction by burning or swallowing. Destruction is an emotive word and can easily be linked to death, to prove that even vegetable sacrifice has as its main aim the death of a victim. This is the claim even of Hubert and Mauss (1964). But did those who sacrificed ever hold that destruction was their chief aim? There have always been more effective methods of destruction than sacrifice, especially when all or part of the sacrifice is eaten – and eating is usually seen as a positive, not negative, act. We must assert that the purpose of sacrifice is benevolent, not destructive.

Thirdly, the material of sacrifice has usually no intrinsic efficacy *per se*. They are common objects. Hens, milk, bulls, human beings do not normally have any wonder-working efficacy when they are not being used as sacrifice. This is how the offerers see them, too. Exotic sacrifices belong more to Victorian fiction than to fact. Domestic objects are sacrificed, usually food. They belong to those who sacrifice and are in close and obvious connection with them. Hence, according to Evans-Pritchard (1956: 479), when the Nuer man dies, his own ox is sacrificed, because it is the obvious 'means by which a man can enter into communion with God'. The Ainu bear is part of Ainu society and is even mourned when sacrificed. In the case of eland depicted in Bushmen rock paintings, this animal, though not domesticated, has affinity with the tribe and its deities. Both hunter and hunted pass through a 'holy danger' period when one is killed (Vinnicombe 1972). Kinship is too strong a term to use of the relationship between the person who makes sacrifice and the thing sacrificed. In any case kinship is hardly felt for a jar of milk! Yet sacrifice is offered from the stuff of life closest to the offerers – their food, their livelihood. Most of sacrifice has always been very ordinary and very much an obvious part of the society performing it.

With these factors in mind, let us examine the motives for sacrifice. Why have people sacrificed? Why do they think they sacrifice? What were the original motives for sacrifice? Is there an Ur-Sacrifice, on which all subsequent sacrifices have been modelled, certainly as far as motives are concerned. Among theories put forward are the following:

1. It has been asserted that universal sacrifice arose out of a universal sense of sin. Hence the original motives are to be found in a deep sense of estrangement from the unseen powers. Sacrifice is therefore offered to them to 'put matters right'. Sin has caused sacrifice, because man knows that he is guilty and offers an animal instead of offering himself. He gives proof that he has offered in the visible blood. The Supernatural accepts the sacrifice and now becomes favourable. Sin is done away with and estrangement changed to accord. It is fairly easy to see the origins of this theory. Suffice it to point out a few difficulties in accepting this explanation as an explanation of the motives behind *all* sacrifice. First, we have to define what we mean by 'sin'. Unless this is done it is all too easy to subscribe to a general definition while placing different meanings on terms used. Sin, in Hebrew and Christian theology alone, can have a variety of meanings, ranging from ritual and legal mistakes to moral lapses and finally to a serious rift between God and man. If the latter is meant, then the question arises of whether it is legitimate to impute such a deep sense of rift to communities which direct their sacrifices at ancestors or other supernatural powers and which appear to express themselves in terms of duties forgotten or threats to be averted? Is it legitimate to impose categories taken from the work of Christ as interpreted by St Paul on pre-Christian or non-Christian rites?

If we widen this definition of the motives for sacrifice and say that sacrifice is performed in order to avert danger threatened from the Supernatural, have we not then answered these objections?

In speaking of aversion sacrifice, a wide variety of emotions and motives may be involved. A threatening power may be being kept at bay by sacrifice. A benevolent being may be being asked for protection against danger coming from another source. It has become traditional in Christian theology to describe the placating of an angry God by means of sacrifice as 'propitiation' and the offering of sacrifice as a plea to a benevolent deity in order to ask him to remove the offence as 'expiation'. Propitiation has acquired a bad reputation in many quarters, presumably because it implies the bribing of an angry God: expiation has remained acceptable. Yet it is very doubtful whether these two motives can be separated so easily in sacrificial practice. If you fear disaster and offer sacrifice to those Beings who are capable of suspending that disaster, it will be very natural to assume that those Beings are angry before sacrifice and placated after it, no matter how much the dealing with the offence rests with their benevolence. All that can be assumed about an aversion sacrifice is that the ingredients in such an action are people who feel themselves to be in danger or are conscious of a vital relationship with unseen power that has been ruptured, or think that they have neglected powers more powerful than themselves.

There is a yet more radical question to be put against the idea that all sacrifices are done *au fond* for the purpose and motive of aversion. Many sacrifices in many cultures do not appear to have any conscious piacular purpose at all. Many West African sacrifices are offered when the harvest is safely in, for purely grateful motives. This applies to most sacrifices offered in India and many Old Testament sacrifices. Harrison's (1922) classification of ancient Greek sacrifice into two distinct types – aversion (*apotropē*) and service (*therapeia*) provides added support. It is possible to claim that though people did not consciously have aversion in mind when they sacrificed, it was unconsciously there, or had originally been there. It is equally impossible to prove such a claim, since either the people and their records are not there to consult or they have to be told that they are acting for different reasons from those they believe in. It is not academically legitimate to twist expressed motives or assume unexpressed motives to fit in with presuppositions. We may only assume that sacrifice *may* deal with a tangle of mixed motives expressed by the words expiation, propitiation and aversion.

2. The theory of totemic union in sacrifice involves the sharing (by eating or drinking) of the flesh and blood of a sacred victim. Through sacrifice the thing sacrificed became divine and then gave divine powers to the offerers as they ate. They 'ate the God' and gained his power. This theory was strongly backed by Frazer in his monumental *Golden Bough* (1907–15) and supplemented by instances of warriors drinking the liquid remains of dead chiefs in order to inherit their vigour. In turn Freud's influence was to be found and in both works there is a desire to explain (away?) Jesus Christ's death as an instance of the 'theanthropic sacrifice of a God'. The Greek rite of the Bouphonia served as another example and as an influence (to put it mildly, unproven) upon Semitic sacrifice. In the Bouphonia, according to Frazer, you 'become Bacchus' through union with the God in totemic sacrifice and thereby manipulate the mana from the God. Unfortunately Robertson Smith took up this theory in his seminal work, *The Religion of the Semites* (1889: 227, 368, 395) and applied it

through 'Nilus's camel' to Semitic sacrifices. Now Nilus's camel is rather like Piltdown man. It is based on the account of a Christian monk who watched Arabic tribesmen carve the flesh off a living camel and devour it. The veracity of the incident has been severely questioned as (ironically) a Christian attempt to contrast the crudity of pagan religion with the sublimity of the gospel, but for Robertson Smith it constituted a prime example of primitive totemic sacrifice among the Semites and therefore this had to be the original purpose of all Hebrew sacrifice. This ends up (not in Robertson Smith's work) with Nilus's camel as the lineal ancestor of and explanation for Jesus's Cross.

The totemic idea has been taken as the original reason for the communion type sacrifice seen as the earliest and original type of Hebrew sacrifice. Two contributory hidden motives in this theory were the communion meal idea beloved of Protestant Christians as the reason for the Eucharist, as opposed to Catholic sacrificial theories (and Robertson Smith was a Scottish Presbyterian), and the dominant J E D P theory in Pentateuchal criticism, which left P-strand material as a later arrival in the Hebrew tradition and therefore the aversion-type sacrifice prescribed in Leviticus, including the Day of Atonement, as also very late and unoriginal. The Hebrews may well not have known all this and would have been revolted by the thought that, in their sacrifices, they were 'eating Yahweh'. Despite this Robertson Smith asserted (1889), 'The leading idea in the animal sacrifices of the Hebrews was not that of a gift made over to the God but an act of communion, in which the God and his worshippers unite by partaking together of the flesh and blood of a sacred victim'. Frazer puts it more crudely, though not specifically with reference to Hebrew sacrifice, (1910: Vol 4, 231) 'The object of the real totem sacrament . . . is not to attain a mystical union with the deity, but simply to ensure a plentiful supply of food for the rest of the community by means of sorcery.' The buzzing of innumerable antimetaphysical or Protestant bees can be clearly heard.

At the root of the theory is the same assumption, that the lowest motive must be the original one. This assumes in turn that religious ideas and practices are of necessity crude and unrefined, though overlaid with sophistication. Hence if an example can be found of the manipulation of a deity by means of sacrifice, in order to ensure fertility, then this must be the original motive for sacrifice. Yet it is possible that the crude ideas are not the original ones, but later developments, not the root idea. In other words Nilus's camel, even if historically sound, may merely tell us that, once upon a time a certain Arabic tribe had such a low opinion of its deities that they thought that they could harness their power by eating them via a sacrifice. Durkheim, strange to say, once asserted that it must not be assumed that magic produces religion: rather it is truer to say that religion can produce magic. Hubert and Mauss (1964: 5) put it more strongly, 'The great flaw in this system is that it seeks to bring the multiplicity of sacrificial forms within the unity of an arbitrarily chosen principle.'

Not only is the totemic theory based on a very limited range of samples, not only does it rest on a series of assumptions that are hardly more than dubious, but also it takes no account of the many instances of sacrifice where no eating takes place – the whole burnt offering, for example. It also renders substitution sacrifices incomprehensible: Why do the Nuer sometimes substitute a susu, which they do not eat, for an ox, which they do eat? The truth is that for every case where totem sharing in the life of the god could explain the sacrifice, there are many more examples where this theory could not do so. We are on much safer ground if we accept Levi-Strauss's dictum: 'Every sacrifice implies a solidarity of nature between officiant, god and the thing sacrificed' (1969: 71).

3. As Van Baal points out (1975) there is a world of difference between trading and giving. A gift implies that there is a social relationship involved, that no law or obligation can govern the gift which is unsolicited. Trading is contractual, is regulated by laws and customs and implies no social relationship, except in a much broader sense. Hence those who see sacrifice as originally and basically gift-giving and those who see it as trading goods for benefits received (*do ut des*) are assuming very different relationships. The externals may be the same: the dynamics very different. Taylor's theory, that sacrifice was originally a tribute given in order to ensure benefits in return, sees sacrifice as a sort of bribe offered to an invisible chief. The bottom line of this theory is that we can use human behaviour as a model for the divine. Because *we* trade for benefits, give bribes, so do the gods have their price too. There is indeed no denying that many peoples in many places have offered tributes or bribes to their gods, and that this idea has invaded the so-called superior religions too. But is it the original idea? Does it fit all sacrifices? Unless, of course we assume hidden motives and estimates at all points. The question, 'What sort of gods

are they that can be treated in this way?' is surely not a modern one. When Micah questioned whether the God of the Hebrews could be bribed by lavish sacrifices, he was surely not the first person to do so. Again, the least lofty motive may not necessarily be the original one. Sacrifice is surely not just an archaic insurance policy. There is also a further question which is hard to answer – if sacrifice is tribute paying, pure and simple, then what of those predominant types of sacrifice where all or part of the offering is eaten by the worshippers and never reaches the gods' table? Have the offerers come to some sort of agreement, that the gods do not need their offering?

So, if sacrifice is not basically a tribute, is it a gift? Many eminent scholars have suggested this, including de Vaux, Gray and Malinowski. The arguments are very convincing, though they do not completely satisfy the objections concerning sacrifices that are eaten by the offerers. Giving and receiving must be present in sacrifice – this is too obvious to deny. Someone gives and someone receives something and that something can be called a gift. But is this the whole story as far as the meaning of sacrifice is concerned? There must be more to it than that. Giving implies relationship, personality relationships, emotions, warmth, joy. It implies participation. 'To give, then, is to convey something of oneself to the strange being, so that a firm bond may be forged' (van der Leeuw 1938: vol 2, 351). Giving sets action and relationship in motion and initiates or continues communication. We can go further than this and see gift-giving in sacrifice as setting the stream of life flowing, as taking part in the circle of creation. This is indeed the way sacrifice is seen in some Indian rituals. To describe sacrifice as gift-giving is not inadequate, but is the threshold of further discoveries. The gift will take us further on into giving, receiving and relating.

4. Durkheim and others virtually see sacrifice as the means by which both society and the gods are maintained. The performance of sacrifice increases faith in the gods to whom it is offered: it thus 'maintains them', because without the faith of society in them they would cease to exist. In turn, they maintain the life of the community that worships them and the fortunes of both the offerer and the receiver fluctuate in proportion to each other. 'The gods would die if their cult were not rendered' (Durkheim 1954: 346). Sacred beings, though superior to men, can live only in the human consciousness. Thus the real sacrifice offered is the worshippers', that is the com-

munity's thought. This, in turn, creates divinity. These ideas are highly sophisticated and light years away from the mind of anyone who has actually offered sacrifice. The offerers of sacrifices do not see themselves as a society for the creation and maintenance of deities or even of maintaining, by means of sacrifice, the society they themselves belong to. Whether it is legitimate to impute motives to people who show no consciousness of them is a problem for psychologists. Suffice it to say that it will be very hard to find any society that seriously thinks that by offering sacrifice it is keeping its gods going and that, unless it does so, they will die and the society will die. 'The school of Durkheim has not resolved the ambiguity of sacrifice by invoking the *deux ex machina*, "society", whom they have placed on the throne of the God who is dead' (Turner 1977: 212).

Nevertheless, Durkheim's point of view does have something positive to offer. Sacrifice is only meaningful if there are supernatural beings to offer to, and, although sacrifices are sometimes offered by individuals for individuals, a community is presupposed. There must be people and there must be divinities. The act of sacrificing is concerned with relationships and it does something to the offering community. 'Thus it becomes the sacred that subsists in common, producing a strengthening of the community's power and binding its members more firmly to each other' (van der Leeuw 1938: 357). Sometimes the sacrifice itself, the action of sacrificing, seems to be almost more of a reality than the gods themselves. It is almost as if the two extremities of the sacrificial offering – the offerers and the recipients – have been, as it were, sucked into the middle so that gods and men and the relationship between them become one mighty act of sacrifice. According to Levi (1966), the Brahmanas represent sacrifice as being an action in eternity. Sacrifice is creation, the means through which the gods have effected their enterprises. In other words sacrifice is the action of the gods into which man enters. The gods subsist on what is offered to them from below just as men subsist from the gifts that come to them from the heavenly realm. This somewhat tropical language describes quite mundane offerings, such as jugs of water, burnt wood, milk, and sacred study. The stuff of this world becomes the communication with the gods, with the stuff of immortality. Cosmic action is worked out in the common coinage of sacrifice. Now clearly Durkheim and the Brahmanas do not mean the same thing when they assert that the gods are maintained by sacrifice. Yet each is pointing to the value of sacrifice, that cosmic relationships are cashed out in this valuable coinage of sacrifice. Man in society communicates in this mode with the supernatural world beyond it in the deepest possible way – and both would die without sacrifice.

5. At the opposite pole to the theory that all sacrifice was originally piacular is the theory that it was basically a joyous meal. This theory was popularized by Julius Wellhausen and taken further by Robertson Smith as a kind of accompanying theme to Nilus's camel. Sacrifice is a clan feast and strengthens the bonds of society. Union with the divine is still the deepest aim and effect, but the uniting of all parties concerned is brought about by 'communion in the sacred flesh and blood' (Robertson Smith 1889: 368). In common with Durkheim the original state of man is seen as man-in-community. The difference in approach lies in the approval expressed by Durkheim and modern sociologists for this approach. For Wellhausen it is a matter of disapproval. By him the individual was seen as having been submerged in the community life and thereby suppressed as to his personality. Wellhausen saw the Israelite prophets as the liberators of the individual from the dominance of the tribe. This liberation he saw as carried through to its triumphant conclusion in Jesus Christ and jealously defended by Protestantism. Sacrifice is therefore seen as an outmoded community-building mechanism, binding gods and men together and adding to the suppression of the individual's free conscience. Not all those who have held this view have been influenced by such motives, and, indeed, reaction against a piacular view of the Eucharist has sometimes been the motive; but it is one-sided.

Certainly the *thusia* type of sacrifice (to use a distinction in the Greek tradition, though not necessarily acceptable in other traditions) had that character. But the aversion types of sacrifice are not necessarily secondary. In any case, how did piacular sacrifices arise out of a tradition in which sacrifices were joyful communal meals? 'The union between God and man constitutes the goal of prayer and sacrifice' (Cassirer 1973: 275). At its most explicit the communion-only theory gives the impression of happy fellowship between gods and men brought about by a Valhalla-like feast. At its least explicit it makes virtually no distinction between sacrifice and any sort of meal. To say that sacrifice is essentially a meal is very necessary, and the liturgical movement of the fifties and sixties worked hard at this, but to reduce all sacrifices to suppers is a mental leap of the same sort as the 'all cats are grey because cats are grey in the dark' type.

6. Van Gennep (1960) defines a *rite de passage* as a rite that takes place at crisis points in life and enables the person or persons concerned to survive a period of 'holy danger'. It is quite common in our own times to rate certain transition events (birth, marriage, moving, divorce, bereavement, change of occupation) as periods of greater or lesser stress. This is not the first society to realize this. Yet in earlier times, these events were seen as times of risk from the unseen powers that presided over life and as events in which the whole community was involved and contributed. Many anthropologists have studied these *rites de passage* which are celebrated on such occasions by the tribe or society concerned. Circumcision rites are among the most obvious of these and especially relevant to us since they usually involve the offering of sacrifice and may themselves be the vestiges of a sacrifice – the blood of the foreskin being *pars pro toto*, a substitute for the sacrifice of the whole person. Edmund Leach (1975) points out that the change of status of a person or of a society involves passing into a 'holy' state, in a sense outside the normal time sequence and outside that society, before achieving the new status. At the danger point of separation from a status A and aggregation into status B, rites are required, purification is needed – a separating off of pure from impure. Semitic sacrifices give many examples of this process. This is certainly a most helpful explanation of the occasions and some of the procedures of sacrifices. The sense of 'holy danger' may not be the right way of expressing this, however. Sacrifices are usually so common and frequent that there is little sense of oppression or danger associated with them. Also it involves some special pleading to classify all sacrifices as *rites de passage* and here we may have reverted to the old game of saying, 'if they do not appear to be so *now*, then this is because everyone has forgotten that they once began in that way'. The *rite de passage* theory does explain a great deal, especially about the sacrifice of the Cross.

7. René Girard has recently (1981) put forward a theory that, before judicial systems were established, sacrifice evoked as a means of coping with violence. 'Sacrifice came to a primitive society, deprived of a judicial system, as the only way of preserving itself against violence, as it diverted to a victim that violence which threatened to strike the members of that society'. (Girard starts from the sacrifice of Christ, which he sees as channelling the violence of humanity on to himself and thus removing it.) Tempting as this

theory is for Christians, it only explains that one instance and assumes that in all other sacrifices there exists sublimated or diverted violence. It also assumes that an act of sacrifice is actually experienced (or was at one time experienced) as a release of violence. But did the priest release the violence of society when he performed the daily sacrifice in the Temple? Does sacrifice necessarily become otiose when there is a developed judicial system?

A further development of the two theories just described is J. H. M. Beattie's interesting approach (1980: 36). He sees sacrifice as essentially cathartic. He describes it as the enactment, through ritual, of the whole process of crisis and redress, through the symbolization and mimesis of traditional causes of trouble and feelings associated with it. He would, doubtless, not claim that catharsis explains all sacrifices at all times, but speaks of the cathartic element in sacrifice, which is also concerned with contact with God, or with keeping the divinity at bay, or with gaining power for the sacrificers, or with neutralizing power already evident. Catharsis is basic to life and sacrifice is concerned with the basis of life in community, even though many instances of sacrifice may not seem to the participants to be particularly cathartic or concerned with the aversion of human violence.

De Heusch's rather involved study, *Sacrifice in Africa* (1985) (with a leopard pictured on the dust jacket that has no connection with any rite described in the book itself) attempts a structuralist approach. The essence of all sacrifice is surrogation. The real intention of sacrifice is to immolate the god. Since he cannot be immolated, being divine, the sacral king becomes the surrogate. Since the king cannot be spared, a 'royal' animal is surrogate for the king. De Heusch collects various examples of these animals such as the pangolin in Zaire and the ground hornbill in KwaZulu. The theory has interesting possibilities with regard to the role of the Messiah (-Servant?) of later Hebraism and with regard to Jesus' role as Messiah. But the theory raises more problems than it solves. What of the many tribal societies in Africa alone, where there are no indications of sacral kingship? Can we accept this as a universal principle underlying all sacrifice, even if this is limited to the African constituency? Do we not need in any case a global structure, with some sort of identifiable evidence from those societies where there is no conscious link between the animal sacrificed, the king and the god?

What do all these theories tell us? We have clarity over the essential actions of sacrifice, over the offerings and over the parties involved. But why sacrifice? Comparisons between the cultures are very difficult to make, since all sorts of factors enter in. Except if we adopt a totally structuralistic view it is not at all easy to compare, say, Hebrew temple sacrifices of the period of the monarchy with those of Hindu temples in India of the present century – or the death of a ground hornbill in KwaZulu, with the death of Jesus Christ. Original purposes of sacrifices are not easy to determine. Even where we have well-documented evidence we have only the belief of contemporary people or the beliefs of the period at which the liturgy was fixed, to work with. To find out why the first sacrifice was offered is beyond the reach of any research. It is lost in the mists of time. Sacrifice is very old indeed. In studying it we are studying the roots of society, the roots of religion, the roots of man himself. Motives (known or assumed motives) and occasions of sacrifice cross and re-cross each other and overlap in every culture and across cultures. 'The same mechanism of sacrifice can satisfy religious needs the difference between which is extreme' (Hubert and Mauss 1964: 60). It would be well to avoid any narrow definition of the purpose of sacrifice and to heed Loisy, 'Sacrifice is a whole world of varied rites, used for many purposes, which by virtue of their continued performance across the ages have never ceased to transform themselves together with the religions of which they were part' (1920: 2).

There are certain salient features of most sacrifices which should be mentioned here in the wider sacrificial context, before they are also explored in connection with Hebrew and Christian sacrifice.

First, there is the use of blood. In the context of sacrifice, blood is tied in with life and its use in sacrifice involves death. It is a life-and-death substance. At the visible level, blood poured from a bowl, or flipped by the fingers, or smeared on a certain stone is the visible proof that the sacrifice has actually been offered. Beyond this, sacrificial blood is sacred. Of all the physical elements in an animal, blood has been seen as the special gift of the gods and therefore most suitable for rendering back to them. It is powerful, because it has this quality. The extreme expression of this idea is in the Dracula legend, where blood is drunk to gain power. At the opposite end of the scale lies the kosher tradition in which blood may *not* be consumed, because it is sacred. Blood is sacred and belongs to the gods, so it is given to them in sacrifice: it is not to be shed wantonly by human beings, so murder is forbidden: it is dangerous to handle, so the blood of menstruation has taboos attached to it in certain cultures. Blood often becomes shorthand for sacrifice. It is in this context, not a purely medical one, that the equation 'blood = life' is made. 'The blood contains the soul of the sacrifice, it soaks into the ground and so is absorbed by the spirits' (Parrinder 1954: 89). It is the blood *sacrifice*, not simply blood, that creates a bond between the deity and the sacrificer in the blood covenant. What the sacrifice is intended to do, the blood will do, since it is the active, operative, sacred, powerful element in the sacrifice.

Secondly, there is the practice of human sacrifice. The assumption is frequently made that human sacrifice is the original form and that all other offerings are surrogates for the immolation of a human being. The very term 'human sacrifice' is misleading, since it covers a wide variety of practices and inevitably conjures up images of innocent victims and cruel gods, venal priests and last-minute rescues. There are many practices which have been classified as human sacrifice which may not be such at all – such as head-hunting, cannibalism, the obtaining of vital organs from living human beings for medicinal purposes, the killing of prisoners of war before the tribal gods. Similarly, the practice of Suttee and of Thuggee and the burial of household servants alive in ancient Egypt may or may not be sacrifices. In fact human sacrifice has only been practised sporadically in history and many cultures that have a living sacrificial tradition involving animals appear never to have sacrificed humans. Of the most lurid examples this may be said by way of explanation rather than palliation. In discussing the gruesome finds at Tenochtitlan in Aztec Mexico, Ingham (1984) points out that sacrifices were of prisoners of war and of young children and that they were a tribute to the gods and to the state, their deaths being part of the process of subjugation. Similarly it has been suggested that the children offered to Moloch in Canaanite rites were still-born babies. The horror of the Israelite prophets was directed primarily against apostasy rather than on humanitarian grounds. Human sacrifice is not to be assumed to be the original or most developed form of sacrifice, but an aberration with a relatively rare occurrence. It may be that human sacrifices, where they occur, are a *more*, not less, sophisticated form of sacrifice and that they have arisen out of a false logic – that the gods will listen better, respond better, the more human the sacrifice. It is interesting that two speakers at the Valcamonica symposium in 1972, Makkay and Radmilli, deduced evidence of Neolithic child sacrifices in

Europe and attributed this to a *developed* (not primitive) culture. Before human sacrifice be apologized away it is salutary to remember that Christianity is founded upon an event that can hardly be described as anything but a human sacrifice!

Thirdly, there is the question of substitution or surrogation. Are sacrifices usually substitutions? In the older debates, the air used to be filled with theological backfirings. A certain school of Christian theology preferred to see Jesus as a substitute for man in his sacrifice, rather than a representative. Now a substitute is not necessarily a representative: if a substitute has to replace a player in a team game, he has his own style and methods and he may even turn out to be a more useful member of the team than the one he has replaced. A representative should only carry out the functions and policies of the person he represents. This is the function of an ambassador, who may privately disagree strongly with the government he represents, but must officially not diverge from its policies. The implications of the substitutionary theory of Jesus' sacrifice are that man is totally unable to provide any sort of offering *or representative* to offer to the angry God, by reason of his innate sinfulness – all his offerings or representatives would be equally sinful. So *God* has provided a substitute, totally different because of sinlessness, and he collects the full benefit of the wrath intended for man.

Now this theological distinction, whether valid or not, should be left out of the discussion of sacrifice as a whole. Fortunately modern anthropology has come to the rescue with theories of surrogate sacrifices – animal for king, king for god, as described above. In sacrificial rites the offerer makes some gesture of identification with his offering whether he is going to complete the liturgy or not. This gesture, sometimes only the placing of the hand on the animal's head, can mean only, 'This one is my sacrifice'. It can also mean, 'This one represents me' or 'This one is to be sacrificed instead of me'. What is abundantly clear is that there is a vital connection between sacrifice and the provider of the sacrifice. The animal, or the vegetable, is an extension of the life and personality of the person or clan that offers. It is obviously not the same as the offerer but then neither is it totally unconnected, provided from outside. Abraham was set a strange precedent when a ram that presumably was someone else's property was provided for him to sacrifice. There is as much disagreement among the anthropologists as to the exact description of the bond between offerer and sacrifice. But all seem agreed that the nexus is close and serious. 'In sacrifice some part of a man dies with the victim' (Evans-Pritchard 1954: 29). 'He who makes a sacrifice, sacrifices his property, that is, himself. The sacrificer gives himself in and with his offering, and in this surrender the offering assists him' (Van der Leeuw 1938: 355–6). As far as literal substitution goes, there is little evidence that offerers are conscious that by rights they should be offering themselves. Levi (1966) has claimed that there are instances in Brahmanic sacrifice where a horse is substituted for a human being. As we have seen, others would claim that sacrifices are substitutes for certain human functionaries or for a god who cannot be sacrificed. There are indeed many cases of much simpler substitution – a less valuable possession for a more valuable one, ranging from the Torachic redeeming of firstborn humans and valuable animals by the offering of less valuable ones, through to susus in place of oxen. But is this theory of sacrifice, ancient or modern, elevated into a principle and then implanted by later generations of either law-makers or scholars into the pre-consciousness of all sacrificers? Perhaps this is where the structuralist approach has most salutary correction to offer. 'The rite is prior to the explanatory belief' (Leach 1968). Even if this does not prove that there is an archetypal structure to all rituals, upon which all explanations are glosses, it does present a useful warning against accepting general rationalization.

Fourthly, what distinction can be drawn between sacrament and sacrifice? The Latin words mean respectively 'a making holy' and 'what has been made holy'. The second is the end-product of the first. Christian definitions of the difference between the two terms tend to be cut out to fit the theological approaches of those who use them (e.g. Mowinckel makes a sacrament into something provided by God and a sacrifice something provided by the congregation for God (1960: 122)). Yet in the context of sacrifice worldwide, it is hard to see whether the distinction between the two words is any more than a distinction between active and passive aspects of the same thing. A sacrifice is offered: the result is a sacrament or sacraments. If the two are divorced, we then have a series of holy objects, without the action that has made them holy. This comes close to magic in the pejorative sense. 'Actually the sacrifice, as such, is always a sacrament. But where it is expressly called so, that is, in Christianity, the concept of the stream of gifts has fused in a marvellous way with the concept of a personal God, and of a saviour who is not only the sacrifice, not only the priest, but also a historic personage' (Van der Leeuw 1938: 258–9).

At last let us attempt some approaches to sacrifice that take into consideration the immense multiplicity of cultures involved. There is an immense variety of situations that affect sacrifices, but do not entirely cause them. Also people do not always know why they perform rituals, but this does not mean that their explanations should be ignored in favour of a theory that in effect says that they do not know what they are talking about.

What is common to all sacrifice, no matter who practises it, is action, action taking place between two parties, the one human, the other superhuman. For this action, material is used, usually material that is familiar, domestic to the offerer. Put a group of people and a chicken together: let them believe that there are deities, or that their ancestors have divine powers. Then let the chicken be set in motion so that there is change, a giving and a receiving, a communication, and you will have a sacrifice. Levi (1966) described sacrifice as a ferry-boat between heaven and earth. There has to be a heaven and an earth and a need for a ferry, a need to visit across, to make links, to make contact. Turner (1977: 200), in a most important article, describes sacrifice as a 'many-faceted process of symbolic action', which restores the flow of relationship between the visible human agent and the 'invisible entity usually thought of as more powerful than the offerer and capable of helping or hindering him by preternatural means' (190). Sacrifice belongs to the *liminal*, whatever its immediate purpose, between the visible and the invisible, Sacrifice must both be the product of faith – faith in the supernatural and its power, and it will in turn create faith. Sacrifice, being an action, is effective. It brings about a change and benefits the sacrificer. It is not just a statutory demand ('protection money'). (Of course, like any relationship it can drift into legalism.) Sacrifice is concerned with action in relationship, with communication, with persons. 'Sacrifice is action *par excellence*, sacred action, mystically efficacious' (Loisy 1920: 9). The deity by himself is not sacrifice, nor are the human beings who offer it, nor the thing offered, by itself, nor the liturgy. The climax of an animal sacrifice may well be the death and the blood shedding. But it is in fact the means, the gate through which relationship flows in both directions. Since one of the parties involved is divine (even in the case of Roman or Greek emperor worship, Price (1890) has argued convincingly that sacrifice offered to an emperor had the effect of divinizing him and his authority, and that even so, the term *divus*, not *deus*, was used of the emperor, a nice distinction probably wasted on his Christian subjects) then sacrifice is concerned with ultimates, with man and God and the relationship between them. It is both spiritual and physical, since it uses material objects, the stuff of life.

What, then, is the coinage of sacrifice? It is an ancient language through which relationship is established and maintained, and communication between the human and the divine carried on in material things. Sacrifice is not man-centred, devised to satisfy certain human needs. Sacrifice, implanted from ancient times in human consciousness so that people performed it without knowing why they did so or why the forbears had begun to do so, is the stated means of converse between God and man, in which the transferring of the thing sacrificed into the domain of the holy is the action through which that most powerful conversation of all flows, the dialogue between God and man, man and his gods.

THREE

SACRIFICE IN THE HEBREW TRADITION

The Old Testament abounds in references to sacrifice; there was certainly an elaborate and intricate sacrificial system in full swing by the time of the New Testament. Although the institution outwardly ceased abruptly after the destruction of the Temple in AD 70, it would be hard to deny that every Jew in succeeding times knew what sacrifice was and knew in greater or lesser degree the traditions about sacrifice handed down as from Moses. He would be uninterested in Greek or Roman sacrificial rites and would regard them as pagan and, if indulged in by Jews, apostate. Jesus was a Jew: he attended the Temple and did not criticize the sacrificial cult as such. Most of the very early Christian converts were Jews. On this score it is not rash to claim that no other sacrifices apart from those of the Hebrew tradition would have had any influence upon the development of Christian thought and practice with regard to the sacrifice of Jesus and to the meaning of the Last Supper in the initial stages. We shall return to this assumption later. At least we can admit that the case for a good understanding of Semitic sacrifice is very strong indeed. It means everything to the understanding of sacrifice in the New Testament. Whatever the actual language of the New Testament was, the thought forms, idioms, practices described, images used, theological ideas are all predominantly Hebrew. In the area of sacrifice they are totally Hebraic. It is vital to investigate what sacrifice, practised by Semitic peoples and by Hebrews in particular, was. Kaufmann (1961: 110) described the origins of Hebrew sacrificial forms as lost and irrelevant. He also described them as 'part of Israel's legacy from paganism'. This is simplistic and tendentious. The origins are indeed lost, but the 'paganism' from which they came was, if anything, a Semitic paganism. Better to say, with Rowley (1963: 71-72), 'It is probable that no simple theory can express the first meaning of sacrifice, and that it was already of complex significance so far back as it goes.' Although there are certain elements which point to a Mesopotamian origin for Hebrew cultic rites (Parrot, for example, thinks that Ezekiel's temple had as its model a ziggurat (1957: 64)), the overwhelming body of evidence points to Canaanite influence. Carthaginian sacrifices, of which we have evidence in the 'Tariffs' of Carthage and Punic Marseilles, share the same names as the Hebrew communion-type sacrifice (Langdon 1904; Gray 1957; Kapelrud 1965).

We are dealing with a long and complex period of history for which there is not much evidence outside the Bible and for which the biblical evidence raises more problems than it solves. The Hebrews settled among already established Canaanites. These Canaanites in turn were related to their more sophisticated neighbours at Ugarit and in the other Phoenician ports. Evidence from Ugarit comes from the period before Hebrew settlement in Canaan, whereas that from the Punic colonies including Carthage from a period after that of the development of Hebrew rites. The Canaanites known to the Hebrews may well have shared Ugaritic or Tyrian ritual, but at a much simpler stage. How much the Hebrews brought with them from the desert, or from anywhere else, will remain a mystery. It does at least seem very unlikely, if only from the design of Solomon's Temple, that the Hebrews at the beginning of their settlement in Canaan reacted *against* the cultic practices of their new neighbours and rejected them altogether. As the story of the settlement itself becomes more and more complex, so also does a total break between Canaanite cult and Hebrew cult become more and more unlikely, if not impossible. What seems most likely is that traditional sacrificial rites were adapted to the rites found operating at shrines in the new situation. In any case it is illegitimate to stigmatize either Canaanite sacrifices or Hebrew ones as 'pagan', since an emotive term is being introduced and the question being begged. What was 'pagan' to a Hebrew in Canaan in the period of Judges? It would seem that, since the materials used in sacrifice were very much part of normal life, and since the semi-nomadic Hebrews were adapting themselves to a new way of life in a strange land, they would naturally adopt the materials of sacrifice and the ways of offering them from the people of the land. This becomes more probable with every new insight or theory about local groups entering the covenant community or about widespread 'workers' revolts' in the Near East at the time of the settlement. It was the 'other gods' who were 'pagan', not the sacrifices. Hence the attack on Baal worship in the period of the early monarchy and the condemnation of Moloch worship in the later monarchy would concentrate on apostasy, the worship of the other gods, and would only single out for special attack those rites which were most typical of Baal or Moloch worship, such as child-sacrifice and fertility cults. There is a suggestion of the smear tactic about the singling out of aspects of religious practice and dubbing them as 'pagan'. This has been done occasionally by New Testament scholars in the quite different context of glossolalia. Here it has been said that speaking in a tongue was a 'pagan' habit caught from Greek mystery religions, and leading to such frenetic sects as the Montanists. Suffice it to say that there is a whole world of difference between inheriting religious practices and language from the surrounding culture world and, on the other hand, consciously introducing extraneous factors into your religion in order to hedge your bets by increasing the number of gods or efficacious rites in your pantheon. What we should be asking about customs and beliefs which resemble and may be derived from those of neighbouring cultures is – what did they do with what they took over? If this question is asked then it soon becomes clear that there are immense differences between Hebrew sacrifice and Canaanite sacrifice. As Quarello (1965) points out, what makes Israelite sacrifice special is that it is celebrated in the presence of a unique and transcendant God. It is not the sacrifices that are intrinsically different: it is the God who is different. Östborn (1956) goes further in claiming that, compared to the covenant celebrating sacrifices or Israel, Baal worship is purely transactional, a *'do ut des'* arrangement. Though the origins of sacrifice and the various forms can mostly be traced back to the general Semitic Near Eastern world, the meaning given to it was Hebrew. It became the sacrifice offered by God's people to their God. The names for sacrifices in Hebrew are many and in themselves tell us little about the motives and purposes of the sacrifices. With the piacular types we shall deal later. While the various biblical encyclo-paedias and dictionaries have tended to lose the liturgies and distinctions between them in small print, Rendtorff's work (1967) and that of Wenham in his commentary on *Leviticus* (1979), have succeeded in clearly separating off the various types. Briefly, six main sacrificial rituals took place regularly in Israel – the *'olah*, or *kalil*, the *zebach*, the *shelem*, the *minchah*, the *chattah*, and the *'asham*. All of these but the *minchah* were animal sacrifices and even the *minchah* could be. (Numbers 28 gives directions for the offerer to make flour into a 'cake' mixed with oil and salt and presented with incense. Salt is an ancient symbol of covenant-making – 'taking salt together'. The *minchah* is translated by the word *thusia* in the Septuagint. Both Cain's and Abel's sacrifices in Gen.4 are called *minchoth*.)

Each sacrifice began with an offering ceremony, the 'bringing near' (*qareb*) of the sacrifice to God. In all the animal sacrifices apart from the *zebach* there was a laying on of the hand before slaughtering the animal, after which the blood was dealt with in various ways. At the *'olah* it was sprinkled, as at the *shelem*, whereas at the *zebach* it was poured out: at the *chattah* and the *'asham* it was carried away in bowls and then flipped with the fingers. The rest of the animal was burnt or roasted and then eaten in varying quantities, according to the type of sacrifice, all of it being burnt in the case of the *'olah*. In some types the priests received set portions in the days of organized shrine or temple worship. At the *minchah* an *azkarah* (see below) was taken. These names have been long ago translated into English and those translations have found their way into common biblical language via the Authorized Version of the Bible. The terms are not always helpful. Rendtorff finds that the *'olah*, the 'whole burnt offering', belongs to the sedentary, agricultural life, whereas other scholars would link it to the nomadic life. He sees it as a solemn act of homage, which became for a time the offering of the king *par excellence* (II Kings 16.13). Exodus 29 prescribes two lambs, with flour, oil and wine to be offered daily, possibly supporting Rendtorff's theory. Leviticus 1 orders the worshipper presenting the animal to lay hands on it, slaughter it and dismember it; the priest is then to burn it – it must be a perfect male. Wenham (1979) suggests that the basic motives for offering the *'olah* were faith, affirmation and thanksgiving for deliverance.

The *zebach* was the community offering and certainly had the character of a meat meal, a feast, for family and tribal gatherings, whereas the *shelem*, the 'peace offering' (this English term is the result of a faulty etymology, connecting *shelem* with *shalom*) seems to have coalesced with the *zebach* whatever their differences of origin. This offering seems to have accompanied the *'olah* and *minchah* and was in part eaten by the offerers or priests. Hence Wenham (1979) describes it as a festive meal. The *'asham* and *chattah* will be described later on in this chapter.

Deductions as to origins are liable to be hazy in the extreme, especially if they are based on the linguistic derivations of the terms used. The age of the terms is not known, their usage in Israel uncharted until the Levitical codes, which themselves raise complex problems of dating. There is a richness in sacrificial terminology in Hebrew, but most of the words used are concerned rather with saying what had to be done than why it was being done.

Some technical terms should be mentioned at this point since they have been thought to shed some light on the origins of Hebrew sacrifice. First, *lehem happanim*, translated as 'the bread of the Presence'. Was this, as has been suggested, a revealing survival of an ancient practice of feeding the gods by means of sacrifice? It could be translated as 'regular bread' and be seen as a survival of an ancient custom of providing God with his daily rations.

Another suggestion is that it should be called 'facial bread', because it had Yahweh's image stamped on it [*sic!*]. Johnson (1947) suggests that it should be called 'personal bread', as the bread put aside at his own personal table. What all appear to agree about is that the practice is certainly sacrificial and that the name at the least presents problems.

The second relevant phrase, *riyach nichoach*, is traditionally translated as 'a sweet smelling savour'. This has passed over into the New Testament and was used by St Paul, without any reservations, about the sacrifice of Jesus Christ. It might be a survival from earlier understandings of sacrifice. It obviously derives from some Near Eastern sacrificial rites, since in Gen. 8.21, God smells the 'soothing odour' (not one of the most felicitous expressions used by the New English Bible). A similar expression, *talah panim* (lit. 'to soften the face'), is used of sacrifice in I Sam. 13.12 and in Mal. 1.9, which the Septuagint translates as *exilaskesthai to prosōpon*. Was it originally thought of as 'pleasing God', or 'appeasing his anger' and is it a survival of a deep-seated ancient instinct that, when you sacrificed, you were placating an angry god? As with all 'petrified linguistic survivals' (Kaufmann 1961: 111), it is difficult to say for certain what import the phrase had originally. What is certain is that any idea of giving Yahweh his daily bread ration, or of 'sweetening him' by lavish sacrifices, is utterly at variance with Hebrew theology from the eighth century onwards, if not before. Hence Eichrodt's remark, 'It is extremely doubtful whether this conception was still a *living* reality in Israel' (1961: Vol. 1, 143).

Some have made an issue of the two words 'offering' and 'sacrifice'. This is in spite of the use of the term *qorban* in Lev. 1.1 to cover all sacrifices. This distinction seems to have been invented by the redoubtable Calvin in order to restrict the term 'sacrifice' to Christ's once and for all action on the Cross, and to reserve the term 'offering' for the Eucharist, thereby implying that the latter is in no way a sacrifice. Nevertheless there are other ways of combating medieval errors than the fabricating of semantic distinctions in Hebrew. Loehr pointed out in 1927 that even the burning of incense was not just a deodorant but an ancillary sacrifice, a *minchah*, to the sacrifice of an animal. Yerkes (1953) has shown that the Hebrew word *minchah* is translated in the Septuagint by the word *thusia* (used normally for animal sacrifice) in most instances, in many fewer cases by the word *doron* (a gift) and only once by *prosphora* (an offering). Nor is it easy to follow Thompson's argument, that sacrifices and festal meals should be clearly distinguished (1963). After all even Wellhausen asserted that every time an animal was slaughtered, a sacrifice was made (1885: 71). Terms used for sacrifices do not necessarily provide reliable insights into the purpose and meaning of the sacrifices themselves. They may be survivals or vivid and non-literal descriptions or they may be terms borrowed from secular life. Dates of first occurrences do not help either, since, 'the age of the text is not necessarily the age of the rite' (Hubert & Mauss 1964: 106). We have to look far deeper than words to find out why the Hebrews sacrificed.

Let us examine closely three possible motives for sacrifice and the rites associated with them – Expiation, Communion and Tribute.

Thompson (1963: 175) set out to prove that expiation as a motive, if not the principal motive, for sacrifice was very old in Hebraism, much older than was usually allowed, older than the period when it appeared to dominate sacrifice. But he exaggerates. He even finds that the coal on Isaiah's lips was taken from the 'fire of the expiatory offering'. It is much safer to admit, with de Vaux (1964), that it is extremely unlikely that new, utterly new, forms of cult were introduced at the Exile, when the whole emphasis was on a return to true Hebrew religion, and when Ezekiel, the prophet of the Exile, accepts them without explanation and without describing the ritual for them. They may well have been rarer and less prominent before the Exile, and have received greater prominence as a result of a stronger emphasis on *community* repentance instilled into the re-formed Israel by the teachers of the period, such as Ezra and

Nehemiah. Yet 'it is important to recognize that not all sacrifice was related to the expiation of sin' (Rowley 1963: 82). De Vaux has expressed a most revealing insight when he remarks, almost in passing, that since sacrifice establishes or restores good relations with God, then every sacrifice must involve a deepening sense of insufficient or broken relationship with God as Hebraism grew in its sense of the Godward relationship. Every sacrifice must therefore to some extent be expiatory. This will bear further thought. Leviticus 4–5 gives three technical terms for this sort of sacrifice together with detailed instructions as to how it should be done. The *chattah*, according to Moraldi (1956), dealt with purification from all sorts of impurities, ritual and otherwise. It is highly dubious to equate the 'unwitting sins' that the *chattah* was meant to deal with, with ritual sins. If we do so then we are making a value judgment, with ritual sins low down on the list of importance. This was not the way they saw them. The distinction between witting and unwitting is never closely defined but it is doubtless intended to safeguard the solemn warning that God is in charge of forgiveness and that a rite cannot be expected to achieve instant forgiveness in all cases. Impurity included various sorts of ritual, moral and community faults. Kaufmann (1961: 113–14) sees the operation as an exorcism 'directed towards the domain of evil and impurity'. Nevertheless there are very few traces of exorcism in the *chattah* rites so that on this score the *chattah* cannot be dismissed, as Kaufmann dismisses it, as 'a monument to a vanished world . . . a fossil of ancient paganism that died when the religion of Israel was born'. Wenham (1979) translates *chattah* as 'purification offering', in which the sprinkling of the blood was the most important part of the rite, purifying the *place* of sacrifice. A scale of animal offerings (down to a tenth of an ephah of flour for the poorest offerer) is stipulated. The offerer laid his hand on the animal. Part of the blood was poured at the foot of the altar, the rest flipped from a basin seven times on the veil of the Holy Place, on the horns of the altar of sacrifice or, on Yom Kippur, on the mercy seat. The remainder was burnt 'outside the camp'. It was prescribed for after childbirth, after healing from leprosy (i.e. skin diseases or discharges), for the dedication of a priest, a Nazirite or an altar, clearly intended to cope with defilement, not 'witting sins'. Yet the reality of these matters remain vital, since the *chattah* did not become redundant, nor did the *'asham*. Moraldi, de Vaux, Eichrodt and Wenham see the *chattah* as a reparation sacrifice (for a private individual according to de Vaux), though doubtless the distinction between purification and reparation got blurred, whilst the rite itself remained distinct.

Milgrom calls the *'asham* the 'cult and compensation' or 'guilt offering' (quoted in Snaith 1965: 80). Only a ram or male 'lamb' must be offered and the blood *poured* (not flipped) at the foot of the altar, the meat belonging to the priest. It was prescribed for occasions when:

(*a*) someone suspected that he had sinned but did not know how.

(*b*) false oaths had been made in the Lord's name.

(*c*) a Nazirite had been in contact with a corpse.

(*d*) a leper was the offerer.

It is indeed significant that Isa. 53.10 describes the Servant as offering himself as an *'asham*.

The third and most puzzling word is *kipper*. Much argument has been made about its original meaning and much stress has been laid on its grammatical form – a pi'el, intensive, form of the verb – *chattah* is also a pi'el form. It is very questionable linguistics to adopt the hoary argument that, because the verb in its qal form (*kapar*) is used of Noah caulking the ark with pitch, it therefore means, in the pi'el, 'to cover sins' or 'to wipe them off', or 'to remove them'. It is equally questionable to search among cognate roots for a suitable meaning, like an Akkadian word meaning 'to wipe off' or an Arabic word meaning 'hoar-frost'. The original meaning was lost and its connection with distant roots or other forms became irrelevant. It became a technical term and in Hebrew usage meant to eliminate, to cancel or to remove. God, not man, was the subject and the object was some sort of sin or fault. '*Kipper* is a rite of healing for man just as much in things physical as in things moral. It was a matter of obtaining from God new life for a man who was struck down by a sin or a shortcoming' (Cazelles 1958: 316). The sinner is penitent, the priest offers sacrifice for him and God pardons, remits and purifies from sin. Bourassa (1970) sees expiation as a preliminary to and a complement of covenant renewal in blood. This also calls for serious consideration. De Vaux claims that 'it is justifiable to conclude that the *kapporeth* (translated 'Mercy-seat' in the Authorized Version) was a substitute for the ark in the post-exilic tradition, 'for no new ark was ever made' (1961: 300). If this were so, then even more weight is given to the thesis that God has the final responsibility for all acts of *kipper*. All ideas of men, or of priests attempting to propitiate an incensed deity, are excluded from the Hebrew usage of the words and from the actions in the rites described. 'The Hebrew verb expressed a rather detached

notion of expiation, by which due stress is placed on the activity of
God himself and the priest, an activity which is essentially intended to
remove sin and therefore to reconcile man with God' (Lyonnet and
Sabourin 1970: 146).

All this is of prime importance in the consideration of the place
within Hebrew sacrifice of the Day of Atonement, Yom Kippur. This
is in effect two rites – the offering of an ox by the high priest for his sins
and for those of the priesthood, and the ceremony of the two goats,
chosen for their roles by lot, the one an offering for the sin of the
nation and the other let loose 'for Azazel' with the sins laid on its head
by laying on of hands and confession over it (Lev. 16). It is to be
emphasized that the second goat *sheds no blood*. The Yom Kippur
ritual is never mentioned in the Old Testament outside the Priestly
tradition. It is not a commemoration of any historical event, unlike the
other major liturgical days of the Hebrew year. Its component rituals,
apart from the Azazel incident, are also prescribed for other contexts.
Yet 'on the Day of Atonement the expiatory rites of the Jewish
sacrificial system culminate' (Gray 1925: 321). Nevertheless it was
only one day in a year full of many other sacrifices and many other
festivals. The fact that Yom Kippur seems to have gained prominence
at a time when the liturgical year was taking shape and becoming
fixed, is of great importance. It should be seen, not as an isolated sin
sacrifice, but as an episode in the liturgical year, occupying a very
important theological place in that year. The part played by the high
priest is also significant. Previously the king had offered. Later, when
there was no king, the high priest offers the expiatory sacrifice of the
year *par excellence*. Could it be that the high priest offered on Yom
Kippur what the king had in previous years offered in the context of a
unified calendar? This could explain this strange and unaccountable
change in the liturgical calendar whereby a whole new major
observation emerged at a time when every effort was being made to
preserve all the traditions of Israel and not to innovate unnecessarily –
the period of the returned community and the rebuilding of the
Temple. Phillips's theory of Yom Kippur being 'devised in Exile as
part of the reassessment of Israel's relationship with Yahweh' (1970:
184) is very questionable, since it rests on the assumption that the cult
was replacing the Torah as a renewing force and the intellectuals or
teachers involved in the leadership of the Return did in fact undertake
such a sort of reassessment. It is more likely that the king had
previously performed expiatory sacrifice on public occasions. After

the exile two developments took place – the high priest had to substitute for the king and the whole year became a public occasion. In this event, *chattoth* and *'ashamoth* survived in connection with single or personal sacrifice concerned with people or places and Yom Kippur took its place as the right royal act of expiation in a year of sacrifices.

Azazel will probably remain a mystery. Various attempts have been made to explain the word, from Driver's 'jagged rocks' (1956) to Snaith's evil angel, found again in Enoch 8.1 (1967). Kennett's suggestion (1928) that the woman in a barrel in Zechariah 5.5–11 is analogous to the goat for Azazel could be helpful, since beyond the goat and the woman may be some ancient purification myth-ritual. Wyatt's attempted reconstruction (1975) of Ugaritic material (C. T. A. 12) would support this to some extent, though this is a reconstruction of a damaged text. Perhaps we have to accept that Azazel's only recorded function will ever be to receive a goatful of sins. But whatever the function of Azazel, this ritual, together with those described in Lev. 8–10, gives ample justification to Leach (1975) for his identification of these rites as '*rites de marge*' in a larger *rite de passage*. The *rite de passage* is concerned with the aversion of danger caused by various shortcomings which have brought Israel into a danger area. If Segal is right, that the Day of Atonement is a kind of detached preliminary to the New Year Festivals, then it belongs even more to a liminal or danger area. The bullock is sacrificed: its blood, specially sacred, is poured on to the holy area at the altar: the one goat is treated in the same way, the other is impure, unholy yet sacred, and so ends up in the desert, while the community undergoes ritually a drama of dying, a releasing and a rising, the first two actions being performed in the goats. 'In the scapegoat case, we need a symbol for a creature which is removed from the ritual stage but is not separated from its impurities. It is therefore appropriate that the scapegoat should *not* be killed' (Leach 1975). Thus expiation begins the process of the passage of a whole community into real communion with God, celebrated in and by sacrifice.

The origins of the Hebrew expiatory rites are hard to trace outside Israel. They seem to have been, as far as the evidence goes, absent in ancient Egypt and in other Near Eastern cultures of the early period. According to Kapelrud (1965), the king of Ugarit used to wash away impurity with the blood of a sacrificial animal *before* the sacred acts began. This tells us little apart from possible corroboration for a view

that expiation is a preliminary to the main business of sacrifice. II
Samuel 24.15–25 would appear to give a sort of rationale for expiatory
sacrifice – to be used in cases of threat, plague etc. The aversion
element in Pesach will be discussed later.

Hebrew expiation sacrifice must be seen against Hebrew faith, faith
in the God of the covenant. Both the covenant people of God and their
Temple which was the theatre of their relationships with God would
need expiation by blood. In the light of the covenant, expiatory
sacrifice should never be seen as a rival to other means of response,
such as expressions of repentance, but as the provided vehicle for
confession and reparation. For the Hebrews it was the right of God to
forgive: sacrifice was the means provided for, amongst other things,
forgiveness, 'Expiation was not a penalty but a saving event' (von Rad
1962: 270). Yet expiation can never be the end of the saving event.
This is why we can never isolate the expiatory sacrifice from the rest of
the sacrificial system in Israel, even during the period of the
domination of Yom Kippur. For sacrifice is neither liturgically nor
theologically expiation alone.

Expiation, the cleansing of a relationship, leads to reconciliation
and this *also* was expressed in sacrifice. Morgenstern (1953) makes a
similar suggestion to that of Segal, that Yom Kippur began as a ritual
purification of the Temple to prepare for Passover and Tabernacles.
In it, the major event was not the goats or the bullock, but the
subsequent triumphal entry of the high priest, replacing the previous
triumphal entry of the king. This would corroborate the use that the
Epistle to the Hebrews made of Yom Kippur. This is a far more likely
thesis than that of Kidner (1982), who asserts that Yom Kippur dealt
only with 'ignorances'. This would leave the writer of Hebrews
building his case on a Christ sacrificing himself for ignorances!

Christians have tended to be dominated in their thinking by the
expiatory aspect of sacrifice. However there is much good evidence to
show that Hebrew thinking and practice of sacrifice was not
dominated by expiation. Expiation was the first movement in the
great symphony, or the overture to the opera, cleansing sin and
making further communication possible.

The second great motive imputed to Hebrew sacrifice is that of
communion, for which the *zebach* was the rite *par excellence*. The
antiquity of this sort of sacrifice is unimpeachable and it is not only the
celebration of Israel's being with her God but of Israel's being with
Israel. It is the community feast, when the community most feels itself

to be a community. It was a time for 'serving' and for 'meeting' God. (These were the two verbs used by Moses in putting to Pharaoh his request for absence for the Hebrews.) The words refer to a relationship, not a clinical description. Near Eastern feasts and feast-sacrifices were not formal state banquets or dinner parties. Flies hovered around them, dogs roamed on the fringes and kites sat on nearby trees whilst vultures glided on the thermals above. Sacrifice was a relaxed feast where you celebrated freely the relationship with God and with your fellows. You honoured him as the Creator to whom life belonged and at whose disposal was the world and the local community. In addition the Hebrews had come to know their God as the person who was reliable and available and had acted and spoken to people in history. So the language of conviviality, of 'eating with', the language inherited from a succession of Near Eastern ancestors, was used, simply because it was the accepted language of sacrificial feasts. The language was neither literal nor consciously archaic, but accepted.

In this context, Nilus's camel should be given decent burial (see the previous chapter). Devreesse described it as (1940: 220) a journalistic and racially biased concoction, and many others (Kroeber 1920; McCarthy 1969) have dismissed it as unreliable. With this unfortunate animal's demise should go the theory that Hebrew sacrifices were in origin totemistic and that the Christian Eucharist is also totemistic. Hebrews never thought that they were drinking the blood of their God. Jesus neither instituted a totemistic sacrifice nor intended his followers to have one – but a sacrifice he *did* institute.

The *zebach* became, for the Hebrews, above all else, a *covenant* sacrifice, for the Hebrews were a *covenant* people. The context is all-important. This centrality of the covenant, even in the cultus, perhaps especially in the cultus, has been grasped by very few New Testament scholars. One of the few was Westcott who wrote that Levitical sacrifices, themselves based on existing custom (i.e. they were not novelties of the post-exilic period) 'in part embodied the devout action of those for whom the full privileges of the covenant were in force; and in part they made provision for the restoration of the privileges which had been temporarily forfeited' (1889: 228). It is debatable whether there were pre-covenant Hebrews. This depends on what credence is given to the patriarchal covenants – did they exist or were they written back into the patriarchal sagas? What is certain is that once there was a covenant, then sacrifice, like everything else, was within that one dominant relationship of the covenant. This was why the practices and descriptions and terminology inherited from previous ages could and did stay with the Hebrews, provided they were used *within* the covenant. It was only when sacrifices violated the covenant relationship and Hebrews were found to be sacrificing flagrantly to Moloch, not to Yahweh, or when they were using sacrifices as bribes to Yahweh, in a highly non-covenantal way, that sacrifices were called into question. Otherwise all sacrifice was the language of covenant relating.

Sacrifice (according to Wenham (1979) in his extensive commentary on Leviticus, and according to Davies (1977), quoted by Wenham) is concerned with restoring the relationship between God and Israel and Israelites. On the one side we have the covenant, founded upon God's greatest act of redemption of Israel, and the holy safety it brings. On the other side lie the threats to be dealt with – sin, death, exclusion from covenant relationship, disease, uncleanness. These are all dealt with in different ways by sacrifice. This is God's calling and prescription, not man's invention and devising. The sacrifices prescribed in Leviticus are mainly concerned with *cleansing*. This is the way it is seen. For cleansing from unintentional sin, repentance and sacrifice are required, from 'high-handed' (i.e. intentional) sin, public confession and reparation and sacrifice are required.

Circumcision was the near-sacrifice that took a Hebrew through the holy danger period which ended in his aggregation into the covenant community. The offering of first fruits was the ancient giving over of holy, dangerous things to the deity, taken over into the covenant context, bringing the first of a kind to the First of all Kinds, the covenant author. The *shelem* according to Schmid (1964: 126), was the celebration of Israel being 'thy people' and of Yahweh being 'God with you'. This was probably true of the *zebach* as well, as it joyfully acknowledged God's goodness, while the expiatory sacrifice cleared away the hindrances, the sins that stood in the way of the covenant relationship. 'The Covenant itself between God and his people was maintained in force, or re-established, upon the altar of sacrifice' (de Vaux 1961: 414). 'The great achievement of the Old Testament is the inclusion of the whole sacrificial system within the saving events and the fact of the *berith*' (Kraus 1966: 122).

The development of sacred personnel in connection with the cultus has a very mixed history in many religions and care must be taken not to import anti-clerical or anti-sacerdotal prejudices taken from Western Christian debates into the assessment of the priest's role in Israel. In the

Torah there is evidence that the role of the priest as offerer of sacrifices did develop late as an exclusive or monopolistic occupation. An Aaronic priesthood is prescribed as from Moses, yet Moses himself sacrifices and disposes of the blood in the covenant ceremony of Exod. 24.4–8. It seems, according to Gray and de Vaux, that the craft of the priesthood, as contrasted with the charisma of the prophet, grew out of the need in the community for a statutory ministry in things supernatural. The priests were originally guardians of the covenant and therefore officiated at the statutory sacrificial rites at the shrines. Then, when the Temple was built, they took charge of it under the authority of the King, who was the chief offerer of sacrifices for the whole nation. It seems to have been part of the unifying policy of the monarchs, from David onwards, that the various clans of priests, previously associated with certain tribes or shrines, found their place in relation to the Temple cult. This was a continuing process of assimilation, presumably completed by Josiah in his reform. With the end of the monarchy and the rebuilding of the Temple, there grew up a Temple priesthood, led by a monarchical high priest, which, partly because of its accepted position as guardian of the covenant shrine and partly because of the stability it provided by its hereditary succession, monopolized both cult and covenant. This is yet another example of the development of the covenant/sacrificing community. Priests were not merely holy butchers. They were guardians of the covenant and its shrine. The difference between them and the prophets is the difference between what Gray calls craft and charisma, the static and the dynamic sides of the community's life, safeguarding the security of the people of God and the freedom of Yahweh himself.

In the previous chapter, the significance of blood was discussed. Old Testament theology has suffered from the projecting back upon it of Christian theological disputes. On the one hand we are told that blood means 'life violently ended' (Morris (1952), Green (1967), Kidner (1951), Stibbs (1948)). On the other hand we are told (not without biblical authority) that blood is seen as life offered up and life-bringing (Dewar (1955) et al.). As was pointed out, blood is obviously open to this sort of ambivalence. When blood flows too freely, people and animals die, but life is offered up if it is given to God. There are of course many places in the Old Testament where blood is shorthand for murder. To have blood on one's hands is to be guilty of murder. In this context there is no sense of life about the expression at all: it will mean death to the murdered and threat of death to the murderers. However, when Lev. 17.11 speaks of 'the blood that is the life, that makes expiation', it is not referring to murder but to sacrifice. The context is obviously important. Similarly, the blood referred to in the laws about menstruation in Lev. 15 is not concerned with death but with impurity according to the ancient taboos about blood. It is blood in the context of sacrifice that we are concerned with, not in the context of murder or menstruation. In his excellent study of Christian sacrifice, Daly (1978) has pointed out that the Septuagint translation of Lev. 17.11 is 'the blood, *instead of* the life (*anti tēs psuchēs*) that makes expiation'. Whether this is original or a paraphrase, this underscores the Hebrew understanding of blood as, in sacrifice, representing the life given to God. Evidence for the use of blood in other Semitic religions is conflicting. De Guglielmo finds no emphasis on it in Ugaritic rites (1955) and there seem to be few convincing references in Hittite, Akkadian or Egyptian sources. McCarthy, after pointing out what very few definite references there are to the use of blood in sacrificial rites in the Ancient Near East, finds only the partiality of the war-gods of Ugarit for blood. In Greek rites blood is poured out, not for the gods, but for the dead (McCarthy 1969). Connections with Greek cultic rites are historically very tenuous and must go back a long way indeed to find a common source. It has been suggested that the rite of the red cow may be a survival of such a custom. In it (Deut. 21) the blood of a heifer mixed with ashes is used as a purification rite when an unidentified body has been found (Cross 1929).

Blood is the 'holy danger' offering most of all showing the transference of the life of an animal connected intimately with the life of the offerer. It is the agent of sacrifice, and is to be transferred to the domain of the holy, the other Person. The blood will now do what God says it must do. A much more revealing line to pursue is the connection of 'the blood of sacrifice' with the covenant. The phrase, 'the blood of sacrifice' is a Hebrew usage of the construct, meaning the sacrifice which has blood in it, as contrasted with the sacrifice that does not – i.e. the vegetable sacrifice. Whenever a covenant is made, so is a sacrifice made and blood is sprinkled or poured out. In Exod. 24.3–8, half the blood is poured at the foot of the altar and half is sprinkled on the people. 'As for the meaning of the rite with blood in the covenant sacrifice, the authors seem to agree in stating that the blood joins or unites the two parties which are to contract a pact, as is the case in pacts of friendship, where the blood of the one is mixed with the blood of the other so that one life, as it were, is produced' (Lyonnet & Sabourin 1970: 172). 'The blood produces the psychic community of the two parties' (van Imschoot 1965). The sacrifice offered at a covenant making is not an optional extra, added to a legally binding treaty already made, when the terms have been haggled over and settled. It is in fact the most solemn binding part of the whole covenant. A covenant is not ratified by signing on a dotted line but by sacrifice and by the blood of sacrifice. The blood used at a sacrifice has a covenant context within Israel. The blood shed at a *zebach* will ratify, renew, celebrate, give thanks for, the covenant. The blood sprinkled at a *chattah* or on Yom Kippur will cleanse and reconcile back to the covenant. The blood from the foreskin in circumcision will admit to the covenant community. The context of blood is sacrifice and the context of sacrifice is covenant.

The Babylonian *puchu* rite in which an animal is offered instead of the king, or instead of a sick person, has been seized upon as a norm and as evidence for animal sacrifice being a substitute for an earlier human sacrifice or for the sacrifice of the king. Yet all rites involving kings are special in various cultures, since the nexus between king and god and king and people is sufficient to produce an unusual situation. It is not completely certain that substitution is the right description of what is intended to take place at such a sacrifice (see ch. 2). It is not at all certain that human sacrifice was original and that, prompted by humane or economic motives, animals were later substituted. It is likely that the laying of the hand on the offering indicates transference of guilt (Noth 1965). But nowhere in Old Testament offerings does the thing offered 'become sin' as an offering. This is especially true of Yom Kippur, where the goat with the sins is *not* the animal offered. In the New Testament the confusion is caused by the translation of 'sin' and 'sin-offering' by the same word. The fact that hands are laid on certain animal sacrifices that were not sin-offerings and were in fact partly eaten by the offerers, suggests pretty clearly that we are dealing with an action of *identification*, not intrinsically an act of substitution. The action of placing hands on the sacrifice 'manifests a certain union and solidarity between the offerer and the offering' (Bertholet, quoted by Moraldi, 1956: 254). Leach calls this a 'metonymic' relationship between the donor and the sacrifice.

Human sacrifice is a much wider term than first it appears. In any form it was peripheral to Israel and not original. According to Moraldi (1956), the evidence for the practice of human sacrifice in the Ancient

Near East is flimsy, too flimsy to support any contention that animal sacrifice grew up as a rationalization of human sacrifice. It seems now to be much more widely accepted that human sacrifice occurs as a sophisticated practice, not necessarily a primitive one and amongst 'developed' peoples. There is still doubt about the meaning the text in I Kings 16.34, where Jericho was rebuilt by Hiel 'at a cost of' (whatever that means) his eldest son, who is then named, which would not have been the case if it had been child-sacrifice. It may not mean that the sacrifice of a male was required for the building of a new city, parallel to the Basotho custom of sacrificing a male when a new kraal, particularly a chief's kraal, is built. In Lesotho a complete stranger is sacrificed in any case. It may mean merely that Hiel's son lost his life on the construction site, or that he paid for it financially. In any case the inhabitants of Jericho were not Hebrews. The hewing in pieces of Agag and of other prisoners of war 'before the Lord' is an example of a totally different form of offering – the *cherem* or votive offering. This is very unlikely to have led to animals being substituted for prisoners in those days before any Geneva convention. The case of Jephthah's daughter is highly unusual, highly debated, and somewhat peripheral to Israel. It seems to have no parallels in the Near East, though there are analogies in Greek mythology.

The *aqedah* narrative, to which we shall return, Abraham's trek to Mount Moriah to sacrifice Isaac, has occasioned much debate. Despite previous widespread opinion in biblical commentaries, in the form in which we have the story in Genesis 22, it is certainly not primarily a polemic or an instruction against child sacrifice or human sacrifice. Its purpose is not to instruct the Hebrews that whenever they experienced a primitive urge to go sacrifice their eldest son, they must conquer this urge and look around for a ram caught in a thicket. If ever there were a transition from human to animal sacrifice (which is highly dubious), there are many other places in the Old Testament to find this, notably in the Cain and Abel story of Genesis 4. Kilian (1970) (see also von Rad, 1961), claims to have unravelled several threads in the prehistory of the account. He finds a pilgrimage aetiology which attached itself to an old story of a son saved from death by sacrifice, which became a clan tradition, which in turn was taken over into Israel's traditions concerning Abraham. Other commentators have gone further from the anti-child-sacrifice theory (e.g. Barth, 1961, Speiser in the Anchor Bible commentary, 1960, G. E. Wright, 1960, Reventlow, 1985). Van Seters finds three interrelated themes involved in the literary work that is Gen. 22. These are the testing of Yahweh, the calling forth of faith from Abraham, and the sacred place which commemorates Abraham's obedience. Moriah (despite its traditional identification with Zion/ Jerusalem) and Yahweh-Yireh are fictitious places so named to underscore the themes of God's testing and God's providing. 'It is a highly polished story with a number of theological themes carefully interwoven to yield the strongest possible impression with the greatest economy of words' (van Seters 1975). 'The sacrifice is a revolutionary act of God by which he justifies himself and gives for all the future to the representative of Israel the pledge of Israel's distinct blessing among the Canaanites. In this sacrifice man goes through the hardest possible trial. In the sacrifice it becomes apparent whether or not he trusts God and obeys him. By vindicating himself God also vindicates Abraham . . . Sacrifice is ordeal, *Gottes urteil*' (Barth 1961: 18–19).

Eissfeldt (1935) considered that child sacrifice, as recorded in Kings, was originally offered to Yahweh as king and that the sacrifices were in after-years attributed to Moloch (a convenient name) to avoid association with Yahweh. This tortuous conjecture is both ingenious and ingenuous. It suggests that more sophisticated ingenuity is attributed to Hebrews of the eighth century BC than to modern scholars. Moraldi (1956) suggests that the remains of children found in jars belonged to Canaanite rituals and might be the remains of *stillborn* babies. Soggin (1969) suggests that the sacrifices at Tophet were part of a mortuary cult. But after all, the only verifiable form of human sacrifice was that of infants in Phoenician-Canaaniterites; this practice spread to Judah in the later period of the monarchy but was roundly condemned by the champions of Israel's traditional covenant. By the time of the exile it had presumably died out. Not even the extra-biblical evidence points to the original primacy of human sacrifice, for which animals were substitutes in the Ancient Near East.

The so-called anti-sacrificial texts in the Old Testament need consideration in any work on sacrifice. The texts are as follows: Amos 5.21–26; Hos. 6.6; Isa. 1.10–17; Micah 6.6–8; Jer. 7.21f.; Amos 4.4; Pss. 40.6;51.16f.;50.13. The question is – are they, all or some of them, attacks on the whole institution of sacrifice? Koehler says that they are just that. He claims that sacrifice was not instituted by God but merely taken over by man from man – from heathen man. 'For Jeremiah all cult is an unnecessary human contrivance' (Koehler 1957: 194). His chapter heading on this topic reads, 'Man's expedient

for his own redemption'. Weiser's views are more moderate. He
describes sacrifice as 'an attitude whereby man, facing the deity at the
sacrifice, puts himself at it were on the same footing as God and
produces a 'gift'. Hence, in his commentary on the Psalms (1962:
337–8) he claims that the psalmist 'categorically pushes away the
whole sacrificial cult'. Many commentaries on the Psalms have
exploited the suspected rivalry between singers and priests in the
temple. This seems to be more dependent on an assumed antipathy to
sacrifice in the psalms than on any other historical evidence of such a
division. De Cock (1960) admits an attack by the prophets on sacrifice
but attributes this to the association of sacrifices with the pagan
bamoth. Vincent Taylor expressed the approach of the older Old
Testament scholars to the subject when, in commenting on Jeremiah's words in Jer. 7.22, he wrote (1937: 62), 'In these words, and
perhaps in those words of Amos, the sacrificial system is expressly
rejected and the demands of a purely spiritual and ethical religion are
set in its place.' For him and, according to him, for Jeremiah, sacrifice
has no place in the new covenant. Even Robertson Smith, who
devoted most of his monumental work on Semitic religion to the study
of sacrifice, decided that the prophets had no objection to sacrifice 'in
the abstract' (whatever that means), 'but it is at its best a mere form
which does not purchase any favour from Yahweh, and might be
given up without offence . . . . The theology of the prophets before
Ezekiel has no place for the system of priestly sacrifice and ritual'
(1892: 295). Gray (1925: 90) thought that the prophets were attacking
only expiatory sacrifice. Yerkes (1953) finds in the prophetic polemics
an aesthetic reaction to a stockyard-temple. According to Skinner
(1922: 181) the prophets found sacrifice to be unnecessary compared
to right conduct. 'Sacrifice . . . does not belong to the essence of
religion.'

All these diagnoses (still in various forms being perpetuated, since
there still persists a Western and Protestant aversion to the cult in
general and to sacrifice in particular) are open to four objections.

1. What of Ezekiel? This prophet's dates are unchallenged, and his
message does not differ in essence from that of other prophets. Yet he
prescribes sacrifice in the minutiae for the Temple.

2. If prophets and psalmists attacked sacrifice so vehemently, why
does the Torah show no sign whatever of any desire to amend the

sacrificial system, when the whole prophetic message is aimed at bringing Israel back to its Torah?

3. The presuppositions of nineteenth-century Europe have invaded the scholarship of many Old Testament scholars. Sacrifice is written off as unethical, unspiritual, mechanical, materialistic and Pelagian, when we cannot prove that the prophets in fact thought this way.

4. The meaning given to sacrifice is in fact a caricature of what sacrifice was meant to be. The prophets also used caricature (hence Micah's '*rivers* of oil' etc.). The difference is that the prophets were speaking to a community that did understand the real purpose of sacrifice and were capable of understanding what the caricature was meant to convey.

5. Speeches of prophets of the eighth century BC are not meant to be understood in the same way as speeches of the political scientists of the twentieth century AD.

Prophets' speeches abound in what Rowley (1963) called 'dialectical negation'. Lattey (1941) used a similar expression, 'relative condemnation'. Hence a prophetic oracle promising irretrievable disaster to Israel, root and branch, will be intertwined with expressions promising restoration. This is the masterly and dramatic use of language, and cannot be taken absolutely literally any more than politicians' manifestos or lovers' professions. The call from the prophets is to reform sacrifice, not to abolish it. It is sacrifice emptied of its content and detached from its context that is denounced by prophets and psalmists. To have condemned all offering of sacrifice would have been, in effect, to have condemned all public worship – for what public worship was there that was not concerned with sacrifice? The prophets were up against a perennial problem in all organized religion. Acts of the cultus, of any cultus, ceremonial or plain, can easily become a set of duties accepted as discharging the whole of man's obligation to God. When Somerset Maugham's American brewer-tycoon (in *Cakes and Ale*) provides for his eternal future by building an enormous Methodist church, he merely does what the Hebrews and everyone else had done before him – the delusion that you can bribe God is always present. In the one case it was personal, in the other institutionalized. But to see through it does not mean an end to all Methodist churches or to all sacrifice. The psalms themselves were chanted at the Temple cult, whilst sacrifices were actually being offered. There is no need therefore, as Dahood (1968) points out, to detach the end verses of Psalm 51, simply because they prescribe sacrifices, when in the previous verses the psalmist appears to have condemned those very sacrifices. He has not condemned *them* but has called for the sacrifice of a broken spirit. According to Briggs (1909), this phrase means sacrifices offered in a broken spirit, a normal use of the construct in Hebrew, not sacrifices consisting of an immaterial, disembodied spirit alone.

Sacrifice needed no explanation or justification in ancient Israel. 'Sacrifice establishes or renews the covenant' (Wheeler Robinson 1946). Würthwein's valuable analysis (1963) of the 'anti-sacrificial oracles' reveals this clearly. The Lord speaks: he finds the sacrifices that are being offered unacceptable, so he does not hear, he does not see, he hates, and the relationship is broken off instead of being affirmed. The offerers are then culpable since they have broken the covenant in two classic ways – by idolatry which offends Yahweh directly, and by social injustice, which offends him indirectly. They are now liable to be excluded from the covenant community of Israel. The way back is by repentance expressed in sacrifice, not in sacrifice alone. 'By and in sacrifices God revealed Himself. Sacrifices served Him and the people as signs of election and redemption. They were a seal of the covenant which God had made and to which He would prove Himself faithful' (Barth 1961: 26).

In the same way Amos and Jeremiah, when they point out that Israel had not sacrificed in the desert, do not contradict the evidence of the Torah, which attributes the sacrificial system *in toto* to Moses. Nor are they thereby providing a valuable lead to scholars to give a post-exilic date to all sacrifices, including the Passover. They are using the 'dialectical negative' speech-form to show that the whole point of the encounter in the desert was not to inaugurate sacrificial systems but to relate to God as his covenant people. In any case, sacrifices cannot have been offered in the desert on the scale of later Temple custom.

Prophets and cult are never totally irreconcilable, as Ezekiel demonstrates. The context of sacrifice should have been the covenant. When it was not so, then it became a religious mechanism, a mark of religiosity, unworthy of the God of the Exodus and Mount Sinai.

The point may seem to be unduly laboured, especially since the anti-sacrificial strain seems to have died out in contemporary Old Testament scholarship. Yet there is a tacit understanding in some other quarters that the attack of the prophets on sacrifice gives a good excuse for omitting sacrifice from Christian or Jewish belief altogether. This is a horse that will not run, since Jesus in his own ministry followed that pattern of prophetic teaching while affirming the essential truth that covenant is to be expressed in sacrifice.

The Hebrews had no doubt about the efficacy of sacrifice – it was a divine command. 'The codifying of the sacrificial system is not represented as a break with the past so much as a reorganizing of what already existed in an elementary form' (Kidner 1951: 9). According to Yerkes (1953), there were four reasons for sacrificing – to learn the will of God, to co-operate with and do the will of God, to rely upon God for protection in doing his will, and to surrender oneself to God and to his will – or, in one phrase, to activate the covenant. Hence Hebrew sacrifices were related to some particular saving act of Yahweh. 'The various different rites became, like the Passover, memorials of God's saving acts in Israel's history and of the special covenant relationship which Yahweh had established with Israel' (Young 1967: 73). 'The purpose of sacrifice is the life, freedom, joy and peace of God's people' (Barth 1961: 21). Far from being a man-made, Pelagian enterprise, 'sacrifice was, and remained, an event which took place in a sphere lying outside of man and his spirituality: man could as it were only give it the external impulse' (von Rad 1962: 253).

Far from being in conflict, sacrificial communion and prophetic ecstasy complemented each other. The coinage of Hebrew sacrifice, as that of sacrifice practised in so many different ways at so many different ages in the history of mankind, and in so many different cultures by so many different peoples, is that it is the language through which relationship is established and communication carried on in material things. The Hebrews took the stuff of their lives, with which they were identified, bulls, sheep, goats, doves, sheaves of corn, loaves of bread, grains of incense, and related to Yahweh through them. In this relating, the first stage was to cross the threshold of the holy danger: hence the first stage in sacrifice was to remove the danger, carry out the *rite de marge*, to remove sin, to cleanse away impurity, to effect reconciliation. But the fullness of the sacrificial relationship was in the sharing of the joy and power and majesty with and in the Holy. Gradually sacrifices coming from different origins, some of them not even originally sacrifices in the narrow sense, were worked together into one vast movement of sacrifice, clustered around and mostly taking place in the Temple at Jerusalem. All this had been converted into a 'solemn sacrificial system' and was now linked up with the person of Yahweh himself. He was thereby proclaimed as the God who had saved and would save in the history of Israel and as the Creator whose work was expressed in the cycle of the week and in the yearly progression of feasts celebrated by sacrifices. Numbers of family offerings, clan feasts, acts of aversion, of cleansing, became swept in to a vast sacrificial system that eventually expressed the whole relationship between Israel and God.

This is the sacrificial background of Christianity, a religion in which sacrifice expressed the relationship between Israel and God, in the context of the amazing covenant which spelled, 'You are my people: I am your God.'

FOUR

CHRISTIAN SACRIFICE

There can have been few Jews, resident in Palestine in Jesus' time, who had never seen a sacrifice taking place in the Temple. There can have been no Jews who had not taken part in the sacrifice of the Passover in some way or other, and known that they were involved in a sacrifice. There can have been no Jews who did not know of, if not know by heart, the sacrificial prescription of the Torah. Palestine was not a vast country. It was not very difficult for all its residents to get up to Jerusalem at least once in the year, unless they were sick, lame or lazy. The effect of the centralization of all sacrifice at the Temple had not been to remove it from normal experience. There were many journeys made by Jews of all sorts, rich and poor, to Jerusalem. The New Testament is full of evidence for this. The Temple had not yet been destroyed: this was an age when it can be safely assumed that every Jew resident in or near Palestine would be thoroughly familiar with the language and the practice of sacrifice, would know about the various types of sacrifice, would have been present in the Temple when they had been offered and would have contributed to the provision of a supply of animals for sacrifice. It was not remote from them but an integral part of the life of the community of Israel. Jesus was a Jew: he never left Palestine from his baptism to his crucifixion: he was often in the Temple. His disciples were all Jews from Palestine. So, presumably, were all the New Testament writers with the significant exception of Luke. In the New Testament we are moving in a thought world in which, just as the Torah and the Covenant are assumed and understood, so also is sacrifice assumed and understood. However, in the New Testament we are also moving in an expanding circle, which aims to include many people who have no knowledge or experience of Jewish sacrifices and whose own sacrificial practices are different, deficient in Jewish eyes and inadequate. The contention advanced here is that the New Testament writers and early Christian thinkers moved from a world which assumed sacrifice and did not need it explained into a world which did not understand it and lost the significance of it. In this removal many vital understandings about Christ's own life and death and about the Last Supper he instituted were lost.

There is nothing in Jesus' recorded sayings to suggest that his attitude towards the Temple and its sacrificial system was different from that of the prophets. He insisted on reconciliation with one's brother before offering a gift at the altar (Matt. 5.23–24), he pointed out that Corban was valueless if it excused a man from the normal obligation of the Torah (Matt. 7.9–13). He instructs the leper to offer the relevant sacrifice for his cleansing. His disciples continue to frequent the Temple. Even his cleansing of the Temple can hardly be construed as an attack on it and on the sacrifices performed in it. In fact, far from asserting 'the superiority of moral claims over those of ritual' (Taylor, 1968: 68) Jesus accepts Law, Temple and sacrifice and fulfils them in himself. By his sayings he fulfils the Torah, by his presence he fulfils the Temple and by his actions he fulfils sacrifice.

The emphasis in post-exilic sacrifice seems to have shifted to the maintenance of the holiness of the community of Israel. Hence sacrifices of cleansing, of expiation, gradually seem to have acquired a greater importance. It was understood (Mishnah Yoma 8) that repentance must be present in the sacrificing community on the Day of Atonement and Büchler has shown that the defilements with which the Day of Atonement was concerned were not just Levitical lapses, but included idolatry, bloodshed, adultery, contact with corpses and evil speech (Büchler 1928). But the Tamid, the daily *'olah*, was regarded as essential and Sirach stresses the importance of the various regular sacrifices and paints a highly complimentary picture of the priesthood of Simon Maccabaeus (Ecclus 7.31; 50.11–15). All this points to the fact that, despite a change of emphasis in the stress laid on expiatory sacrifice, there was no attack on sacrifice as such either by any stream of Jewish theology or by Jesus himself, or by his immediate followers prior to the destruction of the Temple in AD 70. We simply cannot dismiss sacrifice from consideration in connection with Jesus' life, or from Christian thought on any New Testament grounds; we have seen already that it cannot be dismissed on Old Testament grounds either.

What happened in Judaism after AD 70 is, in one sense, of no relevance to the New Testament unless it can be shown that trends evident later were already in evidence previously. When the dust had eventually settled after Titus's capture of the city, a similar problem faced what Jewish religious leaders remained, to that which had faced their forebears in the time of the Babylonian exile. All sacrifices had to be performed at the one place, the Temple, at Jerusalem. There was not to be any Temple at Jerusalem within the foreseeable future. Yet the Torah enjoined a complex pattern of sacrifices upon Israel. What is more, religious rivals were soon to arise in the form of a growing number of Christians who might well be interested to see how the Jews were keeping their Law. In 586 there had been the hope of return, a hope fed by the words of Ezekiel, who had prescribed and promised a restored and more glorious Temple and sacrificial cultus. This time Judaism was infinitely more shattered and there was no Ezekiel. Hence there is a certain amount of confusion about sacrifice after AD 70. According to the Mishnah, sacrifice could be offered at certain places and of certain types, yet according to the Talmud and to Justin, sacrifice ceased abruptly. Some longed for the cult to be restored: others remembered the powers of the Temple priesthood and hoped that it would not be restored. Those who either accepted that the Temple was defunct or who wished it to remain so found ways of rationalizing the absence of sacrifice. Johanan ben Zakkai taught that 'prayer, charity and penitence take predominance instead of sacrifice' (Mayer 1965, Guttman 1967). But it is essential to realize that this sort of teaching started life as rationalization for a situation that had perforce to be accepted – a remedy for an impasse. J. R. Brown has shown that rabbinic writings continue to discuss lovingly the minutiae of sacrifice and to regret the passing of the Temple. Certain popular customs connected with the Temple, like the Temple tax and certain *chaggim* (pilgrimages) continued to be practised. The idea of the Temple, since there was no actual Temple, got itself more and more 'projected upstairs' in the form of the Heavenly Temple, a cosmic allegory, source of light and fertility (Brown 1938). This in itself was no new development, as several books of the New Testament and the Testament of Levi show. In fact this idea goes back beyond to Ezekiel and possibly to Babylon. Nevertheless, these two ideas – of invisible assets for sacrifices and of an allegorized vision of a Heavenly Temple, while formerly adjuncts to the actual and accepted practice of sacrifice, became rationalizations and spiritualizations devised to cope with an impasse in Judaism – the absence of a Temple where all sacrifice must be offered. It is often said that the Qumran community had rejected sacrifice. They in fact looked forward to a time when sacrifice, according to the Pentateuch, would be restored. In the meantime obedience and prayer would suffice as a substitute. Similarly Montefiore (1938: 483) quotes from a rabbinic anthology that sufferings are more effective than sin-offerings, since 'suffering atones for all sins'. But all these are rationalizations, afterthoughts and, to put it crudely, to some extent sour grapes. Sacrifice continued in a truncated form in the Passover, however this might be explained away, in vestigial form in *kosher* customs, in initiatory form in circumcision, and its passing was in fact lamented at the Wailing Wall, however much later generations might transfer their laments to the building or the nation that had been shattered and scattered.

For the Christians it was a different matter. They had a sacrifice which no destruction of a Temple could abrogate. 'For God designed him to be the means of expiating sin by his sacrificial death, effective through faith' (Rom. 3.25): this is just one example of the language of sacrifice applied to Christ's death and, as we shall see, to his life, throughout the New Testament. Let us attempt to find out what becomes of Christian sacrificial belief and practice.

Christians began as a sect within Judaism, worshipping, which in fact meant taking part in the sacrificial round, in the Temple, using synagogues in the diaspora as the natural places to begin their campaign to proclaim their good news about Christ. The destruction of the Temple in AD 70 must have forced upon at least those Christians in Palestine a need to rethink further their attitude to the sacrificial cultus. Clearly they had less reason to long for a restoration of the Temple than the Jews did. Hence the 'spiritualization' of sacrifice, the replacing of Temple sacrifice with offerings of prayer, praise, and other 'invisible assets', such as was already outlined in Judaism in, for example, Ecclus. 35.1–7, found an even easier expression in Christian circles than in Jewish ones. The term *logikos* began to be used of sacrifices offered by the Christian community, in contrast to the bloody sacrifices that had been offered in the Jewish Temple. Now there are various elements in this change which criss-cross from Judaism and Christianity and from the Graeco-Roman world in which Christianity and Judaism found themselves, for a time, rivals in attracting converts from a dying paganism. For rather different reasons both Judaism and Christianity were religions without an overt sacrificial cultus. Neither religion performed animal sacrifice, the Jews because they could not, the Christians because they need not, since Christ's sacrifice. Soon there appeared on the scene another very strong motive for reconsidering the language of sacrifice. Both religions, from the second century onwards particularly at Alexandria, that great centre of learning, felt the need of an apologetic directed at highly intelligent people of various races, who had come under the influence of Greek philosophy and felt the need for an appeal to the whole man, rather than to their minds alone. For a long time, at least since Plato, philosophers and their disciples had treated the public sacrificial system with an attitude ranging from indulgent tolerance to outright contempt. Plato himself had attacked the bribing of the gods with sacrifices (see Nikiprowetsky 1967: 98) while Heracleitus had expressed a revulsion for sacrifice. Philo, the Jewish philosopher of Alexandria, looked upon sacrifices as a concession to human materialism: he admitted that they were a means of serving God, but emphasized that they must be supported by an interior disposition towards God – 'God's tribunal is incorruptible', he wrote, showing quite clearly that he had accepted the bribery theory of the philosophers concerning sacrifice. Typical of his thought is his allegorization of the Temple, 'Two sanctuaries of God exist, the one being the visible universe in which the high priest is the first-born of God, the divine Logos, the other being the rational soul in which the priest is the true man who has as his visible pattern the high priest who recites the prayers and offers the sacrifices transmitted by our prayers' (Nikiprowetsky: 102). Under the pressure of a growing opinion in the Hellenic world that sacrifice was useless because it implied bribery of the gods, it was not surprising that in the first few centuries of Christian thought, sacrifice was dropped, laughed out of court, never taken seriously. One suspects that the reason why it is still laughed out of court is that it still offends the minds and aesthetic sensibilities of Western theologians, who still suspect as their Greek predecessors did that the only reason why anyone would have ever had to offer a sacrifice was to bribe a god or wade around in blood. It is indeed odd that the most carnivorous nations of the modern world are most outraged by the blood of sacrifice – the blood of the shambles, of the abattoir, being unseen, does not affect them. The motives attributed to sacrifice were just as erroneous then as they are now. Young has proved this point most effectively in her researches into the post-New Testament period (1967). As we shall see, very little is said about sacrifice in early Christian writings. It is perhaps significant that least sacrificial language is used in Luke/Acts, where the author perhaps realized that, in his apologetic to non-Jews, he had better play down what they either would not understand or what might be repugnant to them. If this is so, then may one dare to remark that the mistake was made early on in Christianity?

St Paul uses the phrase *logikē thusia* in Rom. 12.1, and it is to be noted that the context is right at the beginning of the second part of his great 'gospel': he has already developed Christ's work and man's response in faith to it. Now he turns to the way in which faith must be acted out and exhorts Christians to offer themselves to God as a living sacrifice, the worship offered by mind and heart. The assumption is that Christ is already our sacrifice, that our self-offering is in his offering and that ours consists in lives that show that they have accepted his sacrifice. As Moule points out (1950), we have Temple, priest, altar, sacrifice. In him we offer ourselves.

A different development takes place in the Apocalypse, where there is a vision, in Rev. 11.19 and 8.1–3, of a full-scale sacrifice proceeding in Heaven, where the gifts on the heavenly altar are the souls of the righteous and the prayers of men. Now this is not *the* sacrifice that is being alluded to – the sacrifice is the lamb slain, which we shall look at later. This is a different way of saying what St Paul said in Rom. 12.1, that the response of the faithful is offered up in Christ's one true sacrifice, which has already been offered and now belongs to the heavenly, eternal scene, because it is not a self-perpetuating activity but an eternal act of God.

The phrase 'spiritual sacrifice', *pneumatikē thusia* (I Peter 2.5), must also be seen in its context of the whole people of God as constituting a holy priesthood, built into a spiritual Temple. This again is in contrast with the Hebrew Temple, and its sacrifices are spiritual precisely because they are in Christ whose sacrifice is assumed. In any case wherever the word 'spiritual' crops up, there is a double meaning underneath it. For spiritual is both contrasted with fleshly, material, and also means 'of the Spirit', 'in the "Spirit"'.

Whatever the pressures might have been upon New Testament writers to avoid the language of sacrifice, they became greater upon the post-New Testament church fathers. Sacrifices are described as 'pagan', they feed the demons. The *Epistle to Diognetus* ridicules Jewish sacrifices and classes them with pagan ones. Justin maintains that God never needed sacrifices. The anti-Jewish polemic was already developing. Clement of Alexandria points out that sacrifices originally arose because man was carnivorous. He advises vegetarianism as a way of controlling sexual desires (Young: 1967). To take but one example from the later fathers, Theodoret of Cyrrhus wrote that the Hebrews had learnt bad habits during their Egyptian bondage. Amongst these bad habits was that of sacrifice, which God had permitted to them since otherwise they might have gone on sacrificing – to other gods!

Sacrifice, in other words, was for the Jews a sort of vaccination. Much of this is a reaction to dominant philosophical ideas of the time, particularly those of the very influential school of Neoplatonism, led by the redoubtable Porphyry. As Young, in her admirable study of the loss of sacrificial ideas in early Christianity, puts it, 'The basic problem of the Neoplatonists was to explain their sacrificial practice when their philosophical concept of God had rendered traditional ideas about how sacrifice worked completely unacceptable' (1967: 32). The key to this attitude lies in the Neoplatonists' philosophical concept of God, as impassible. What need would he have of sacrifices? In their desire to keep up with the philosophers, Christian thinkers found themselves falling in with current philosophical presuppositions and deducing accordingly. This was by no means the last time that Christian theology tied itself to current philosophical apron-strings. The sacrificial terminology dropped out of Christian thought for a while. Vestiges of it remained in the offerings of first fruits and in 'invisible assets'. Augustine's definition of sacrifice as 'every action done that we may be joined to God in holy fellowship' (*de Civ. Dei* 10.6) did little to help, since it meant that every thought, prayer, alms directed in any way Godwards was a sacrifice. But it was an attempt to rescue the word from oblivion. The causes of the loss of the coinage of sacrifice to early Christian thought were a mixture of Manichaean tendencies, which regarded meaty, fleshy, bloody offerings with horror, the upstaging of Christian thought by Neoplatonism and sheer ignorance, especially after the forced end of Jewish sacrifices in AD 70, of the nature and purpose of sacrifices. The result was a very thin doctrine of the atonement, concentration on the ransom paid to the devil, and a legacy of unsettled eucharistic controversies. As Young has so clearly shown, one of the weaknesses of patristic theology was its inability to take sacrifice seriously. For sacrifice was not rendered otiose by Christ any more than was the Torah. Nor did the Epistle to the Hebrews imply this. Fulfilment of Hebrew religion, not its abrogation, is the theme of the New Testament.

As we have seen, the word *kippur* was probably a technical term for an expiatory sacrifice, with the Yom Kippur as its climax in the Hebrew year. Its context in the Old Testament was exclusively sacrificial in the form in which it occurs (the pi'el). Here we have a problem of language and its usage, since the English word 'atonement', by its very structure (at-one-ment) can cover any aspect of the relationship between God and man in Christ. Hence large tomes have been written on the Atonement which give little or no space to the sacrifice of expiation. Atonement became a series of theories which explain or attempt to explain why Christ died on the Cross. So we have Christus Victor theories, moral theories, penal theories and even sacrificial theories. Apart from the last one, these are not '*kipper*' at all, but arise in one way or another from the reluctance of the early Christians to use the sacrificial terminology about Christ's work. This is not the place to describe at length the various images, judicial, military and legal used by the early Christians, from St Paul onwards, to describe Christ's work. 'As soon as St Paul begins to theorize about forgiveness, his ideas become judicial rather than sacrificial' (Rashdall 1919: 132). The late Dr Sellers used to remark in his lectures that theories of the Atonement could be ranged in concentric circles around what actually happened, but that the nearest circle to the centre was the sacrificial theory. It is, however, essential to see what underlies Paul's explanation of Christ's work written for the benefit of Christians outside Palestine, many of whom, Jews or Greeks, may never have seen a Temple sacrifice at Jerusalem. He was in fact writing to people, Jews or Greeks, who had either never experienced sacrifice at all or whose experience was dangerous. So he uses juridical terms – 'acquittal', 'penalty paid'. The language is that of the law courts familiar to his readers, the thought behind it is that of a covenant broken or being made. He uses commercial terms, – the buying back of slaves, the price paid. The language is that of the market place, but the thought behind it is that of entering into covenant as Israel had done at Sinai. He uses the Greek term of manumitting slaves, but puts into it the Hebrew idea of acquiring a people by covenant. He uses political terms. Christ is the Saviour, the Liberator, 'he quite gratuitously frees us from every slavery, so that we become "his own"' (Lyonnet & Sabourin 1970: 103). In the New Testament, the terms derived from the word *lutron* are taken over from the Septuagint, where they translate the Hebrew words *padah* and *ga'al*, which are always used of a positive act of God. God rescues, redeems, ransoms, liberates his people from Egypt. He makes no bargain for them. He simply frees them. The background to this is God's previous mighty act of rescue of Israel from Egypt. It is Paul's attempt to use the language of the Exodus, of Sinai, of making a covenant people by God for himself, and putting that language in the context where it will be understood by Jew and Greek alike in different ways but with the same end in view – 'you have been excused from sin by Christ'. It was precisely at this point that the early church fathers lost the original background in Paul's thought and inserted instead a background of their own which St Paul had never intended to be there. They made it, not a rescue operation pure and simple, but a bargain driven with the devil – the devil who had played no part in the Exodus at all. In Exodus God had defeated Pharaoh: the fathers had God driving a hard and somewhat immoral bargain with the devil for his people. Almost alone amongst the fathers, Athanasius sees Christ's self-sacrifice as 'an offering to satisfy the demands of his truthfulness. It was a sacrifice made by God himself out of the depths of his love for his creation' (Young 1976: 278). At least Athanasius had not gone on to ask and answer the question, 'To whom was the sacrifice, or ransom, paid?' Certainly not to Pharaoh, nor to the devil, but to God in a reciprocal action in which God is the liberator, the initiator, to whom the Hebrews offer sacrifice. The real problem underlying subsequent christology has been that the original act of Christ was seen and intended in terms of a supremely liberating and victorious act of God in Christ, well prepared for by that supremely liberating and victorious act of Yahweh – the rescue of Israel from Egypt and the making of the Sinai covenant. This is an act of sacrifice, fulfilling the whole of the sacrificial system, the 'liturgical year' of Israel. This is then translated by St Paul and other images are used to put this across to those, Greeks or Jews, for whom the sacrificial system was distant or unreal. The new set of images, borrowed from the law courts or from the slave markets, in turn became the standard language of atonement and, instead of the original language of sacrifice and covenant, a language of the acquittal of guilty defendants, or of the paying of debts or even, later on, of the payment of feudal dues, took its place. Now translation of the idiom of one culture and its reinterpretation in the idiom of another is an ongoing task of the Christian church: few would deny that. Nevertheless, the problem arises when the original images are forgotten, so much that they are utterly denied as ever having been present. This stage has been reached. The language of sacrifice has long since been phased out in Western theology. In those cultures of the present world where sacrifice is well known as a practice, the opportunity to return to the original image has been missed.

A very good example of the loss or misunderstanding of the sacrificial context is furnished by the phrase in Rom. 8.3 translated in the text of the New English Bible as 'by sending his own Son . . . as a sacrifice for sin'. This, according to Saydon (1946) and many others, including Luther, means that Christ became a sin-offering, an *'asham*. St Paul was using a shorthand technical sacrificial term and the Greek was deliberately left as 'sin', because it was aimed at Gentile converts, to whom the idea of a sin-offering would have been foreign. To deny this is to start a quite gratuitous theological debate about the feasibility of Christ becoming sin for us. Of course he did not 'become sin', nor, with Augustine and Calvin, was sin (completely unfairly) 'imputed to him'. He entered the 'holy danger' area as the neutral offering and in him mankind makes its passage from alienation from God to reconciliation with him in forgiveness.

'Later theories of the atonement have resulted from a somewhat uncritical combination of the juridical language of St Paul with the sacrificial language of the Epistle to the Hebrews.' Rashdall's (1919: 150) critique was probably accurate. His conclusion would have been better expressed in a return to the meaning of sacrifice, perceived by Duns Scotus when he maintained, according to James, that the Atonement depends on 'the "extrinsic acceptance" by God [of Christ's sacrifice] rather than its own intrinsic value' (1962: 122). Marcus Barth's crucial paper (1961: 51–53) is a modern attempt to put this right. For him, 'the sacrifice of Christ shows in a unique way the necessity, cost and character of relationship between God and man'. Christ's sacrifice enables man to respond to God, since it glorifies God and proclaims the mystery of the Trinity, shows what is true humanity, is the *rite de passage* itself from death to life, from darkness to hope and is the living link between Israel and the Church. It is the same language of sacrifice that speaks of God's relationship to Israel in the Old Testament as it speaks of God's relationship to mankind in the New Testament.

The rejection of the language of sacrifice by theologians in the West down the centuries has happened for two main reasons. The first was reaction against the medieval popular belief that the Mass was the repeated sacrifice by the priesthood of the Church. The second, in a later age, was the assumption that sacrifice was crude, primitive, immoral or amoral and implied the propitiation of an angry God. In this, as in many other matters, the figure of Calvin stands at a great divide. It is essential to remember that Calvin was fighting a theological battle on two fronts. Not only was he concerned to proclaim the new-found concept of '*sola fide*' but he was also concerned to repudiate any notion, whether from medieval sacramental theories or from the ideas of the Renaissance humanists, that man could in any way pay for his own salvation. On this latter count, it is no wonder that he found such solace in the writings of Augustine, who had fought a similar battle, under quite different circumstances, against the much maligned Pelagius. Hence we find Calvin (*Institutes* Book 4 ch.18, sec. 13–15) explaining the atonement of Christ in terms of a *sacrifice* of propitiation, mounted by God to appease himself in his just anger against the sins of mankind. God does this in order to satisfy himself as the plaintiff in a judgement passed in his favour and against man – to wash away sins. This sacrifice is God's act, done under his initiative, completed once for all and unrepeatable. God provides for mankind the substitute, who collects the anger and condemnation due to the whole human race. The trouble with this is not that it is cruel, or that it paints a picture of God as a savage and raging deity, satisfied only by the blood of his own Son. On the contrary, the difficulty is that one misunderstood Hebrew concept of sacrifice has monopolized the meaning of sacrifice and this together with St Paul's non-sacrificial, juridical language has been allowed to provide a devastating misrepresentation of what Christ did. Nor was any opening left for the compensation of a wider meaning to sacrifice, since Calvin feared that the door would thereby be left open for repeated propitiations accomplished by repeated masses performed by priests who had thereby arrogated to themselves God's work. Hence the eucharist becomes an *offering*, not a sacrifice, and an offering of praise, reverence and thanksgiving, that is, consisting of no physical offering at all, but consisting entirely of invisible assets and connected with Christ's life by the continuing reality of Christ's presence in his church, but which must nevertheless be repeatedly received by it as such. The point has often been made that great polemicists have often been right in what they have affirmed, but wrong in what they have denied. Be that as it may, Calvin's analysis of sacrifice has affected theological disputes ever since in the West, and has obliged theologians to accept his premises about sacrifice and then either to accept his deductions or to deny them vigorously. Few have questioned the premises themselves. This is particularly true of New Testament theology, where apart from Calvinist circles themselves, there has been an almost indecent haste to seek for any other possible image for Christ's work other than sacrifice. Yet is was the original image that inspired Christ and the early church of the New Testament.

First there is the cluster of ideas around the theory that Christ died in order to elicit a Moral Response. Mozley wrote, 'Only . . . where the moral response is evoked through a sacrifice which God first supplies, and sacrifice can be made to do justice to those moral necessities which proceed from the nature of a holy God, can we be made possessors of the active ethic and the no less active piety which together go to build up the fabric of true personal religion' (1915: 30). This sounds tremendous. In fact it says no more than the prophets said in old Israel, that sacrifice must evoke a response and that response is for the covenant community to love God and its neighbour. This was implicit, though doubtless often forgotten in Hebrew sacrifice. 'Don't sacrifice if you don't mean it!' Jesus' death could hardly have been less than a moral response to God. Had it not been, it would have been an accident. Had it not intended to evoke a response from mankind it would have been one of the many acts of injustice that this world produces. But this does not exclude it being a sacrifice. Far from it. It becomes the very epitome of sacrifice. Similarly Rivière creates a false antithesis when he says that Christ's sacrifice was 'no mere ritual symbolism, but a sublime moral sacrifice' (1909: 253). This misses the point of sacrifice, particularly that of Christ. He did not offer a 'moral' sacrifice, but he offered himself. In the same way, it is very doubtful if Christ's sacrifice can be characterized simply as the sacrifice of obedience. If this means that his only sacrifice was his obedience (another invisible asset), then what of the blood shed and the body broken? What came back on Easter Day – an Obedience? Little did Mozley realize the implications of his remark, 'Obedience is the truth of sacrifice; it was so in the Levitical praxis, and it is so in the Cross' (1915: 184). Precisely so, for in both cases, it is not mere obedience which is being offered, the quality of 'doing what you are told', 'yours not to reason why', but the obedience of a people under covenant, who offer sacrifice, because they have been told to and because they express their obedience in terms of mactated animals and burnt loaves of bread. We cannot expect sacrifice to immaterialize itself because we call it obedience. Again, both prophets and covenant had already taught this *ad nauseam*, that sacrifice must be offered in covenant obedience, it was not an automatic bribe to a god whether he be angry or not. It is clear that the ghost of invisible assets such as ethical response or obedience as constituting, by themselves, Christ's sacrifice must be laid. At that time and in that place either Christ's death and life was a sacrifice offered, true, in perfect moral response and in obedience, but consisting of a physical passing across of a physical being through the bloody area of holy danger – or it was not a sacrifice at all, but a legal transaction of some sort or a good example of how to live and how to die.

Two almost obsessive themes have been hailed by many New Testament theologians as the origins of Jesus' own idea of his life and death and its purpose. These have sometimes been combined with sacrifice, but quite often have provided an alternative to any idea of sacrifice at all. One wonders indeed whether sometimes the thought is not, 'We must find some image that Jesus might have had which will avoid our having to take sacrifice seriously.' The first is the Suffering Servant of Isa. 53 and the second is the Martyr.

'If He reinterpreted the doctrine of the Son of Man in terms of Isaiah 53, and saw His own destiny in the light of this perception, He must have thought of His suffering as a sacrificial offering in which men might participate' (Vincent Taylor 1933: 48, followed and preceded by many others). Jeremias even links, as will be seen later, the lamb references with the sheep of Isaiah 53. Further he says that Christ's 'death is the vicarious death of the suffering servant, which atones for the sins of the "many", the peoples of the world, which ushers in the beginning of the final salvation and which affects the new covenant with God' (1966). Much has been made, by many scholars, of the identification by Jesus of himself with the suffering servant of Isa. 53, even to the extent of imputing such an identification to St Paul in Rom. 3.25. A study by Morna Hooker (1959) has done much to explode this assumption. She questions the assumption that in the first century a 'suffering servant' would have been identifiable from scattered servant songs in the later chapters of Isaiah – a product of modern scholarship. She questions the identification of the sheep of Isa. 53 with the New Testament lamb. To these grave objections it could be added that even the Ethiopian eunuch, who quotes from Isa. 53, only quotes v.7, as a prediction, and that verse concentrates exclusively on the lack of resistance of the servant as a sheep about to be slaughtered or a lamb about to be *sheared*.

Many would, however, admit the ancient claim that the title attributed to Jesus by the Father at his baptism, 'My Beloved Son' (Matt. 3.17), is an allusion to Isa. 42.1 and to Gen. 22.16. The Father-Son theology of John could also be based on the Abraham-Isaac relationship of Gen. 22. (cf. Wenham on Lev. 1, 1979). Jesus did claim, after all, that he had come to serve and he certainly acted out the part.

Jesus in fact made no proven identification of himself with the servant of Isa. 53 and even the apostolic preaching used Isa. 53 as a prophecy of the non-resistant sufferer, not as the vicarious sacrifice.

The second theme is that of the martyr. This is a much harder theme to argue against, since, by any definition, Jesus obviously was a martyr and his death martyrdom. The implication in some theologians, such as Rashdall (1919), was that Jesus' act should be seen as martyrdom, for his followers, with no other sacrificial connotation. Somewhat deeper is the case advanced by Downing (1963), who draws on II Macc. 7.37-8 and IV Macc. 6.27-9 and 17.22, as does Vincent Taylor (1933: 45). These texts show that the sufferings and deaths of certain martyrs in the intertestamental period were seen in Judaism as having an expiatory effect for the nation. Hence Jesus thinks of himself as dying for the nation, in expiation for them. 'Jesus is about to be murdered for his nation; but, by the shedding of his blood, God will provide an expiation for the sins of the new Israel, the twelve who have received him.' Downing also points out that the passion narratives have the characteristics of *martyria* (Acts of Martyrs). This is rather a circular argument, since it could be that *martyria* took on the characteristics of passion narratives. There are a few indications of the linking of martyrdom with expiation in various New Testament texts. In II Tim. 4.6 Paul speaks of his life 'being poured out upon the altar'. In Rev. 6.9 the souls of those slaughtered for God's word and for the testimony they have born are under the altar. While the reference to martyrdom and its connection with the heavenly altar is quite clear, it is doubtful if it is to be taken as a clear indication that the martyrs are seen as an expiatory sacrifice at the heavenly altar, for they cry to God to avenge their blood, and the blood of *expiation* does not cry for vengeance. Perhaps the unexpressed problem in the New Testament is the coincidence in Jesus' case of suffering with sacrifice. After all, in the Hebrew tradition sacrifice did *not* imply suffering.

'The sight of blood poured out at the altar did not evoke, for the ancient Semites, the idea of suffering undergone' (Médebielle 1938, Vol.3, col.74).

The suffering of a slaughtered animal was no more considered than the processes of the abattoir are today. In Jesus' case there is suffering. This may well be the clue to the understanding of Col. 1.24 in which Paul writes of himself as 'helping to complete, in my poor human flesh, the full tale of Christ's afflictions still to be endured'. Could it be that Paul does not see Christ's *sufferings* as completed once and for all but continuing in his church and in the sufferings of the apostle himself, whereas his *sacrifice* was incontestably complete and there is no question of anyone adding to that by way of completion? The link between suffering and sacrifice is not thought out, since it had only begun to be considered with the Maccabees and then not fully. Even in the case of the suffering servant of Isa. 53, the sequence of thought is that the servant suffers undeservedly and is condemned to death unjustly and that this event becomes a sacrifice for sin. It is not as if at that stage a simple equation is made between suffering and expiation. In the Hebrew sacrificial system expiation might well have been *costly* in terms of animals offered and repentance shown, but it was not *painful*. This is a new dimension only fully realized in Christ's death, though to some extent prepared for by the deaths of the Maccabean martyrs. It was to lead, in Christian thinking, to the identification of martyrdom, and even asceticism in the days when martyrdom ceased to occur, with expiation. But this in no way means that we can identify martyrdom in the case of Christ with expiation and then remove the sacrifice, leaving only martyrdom. Martyrdom is easier to understand today than sacrifice, and it is certainly true that the New Testament church saw Jesus as a martyr, if not *the* martyr, whether Jesus himself saw himself in that light or not. But martyrdom cannot take the place of sacrifice and we do not wish away the problem of Christ's death by calling him a martyr.

The only full-scale treatment of sacrifice in the New Testament is to be found in the Epistle to the Hebrews, which has acquired a rather unfair reputation as a 'high church' epistle, concerned with priesthood, sacrifices and the Temple. Yet it is essential to see that these are not the central themes of the epistle. It is concerned with moving on from first principles to the person and office of the redeemer, who has perfected everything, including the cultus, in himself (William Manson 1951). The chief tool of the author's argument is likewise not the cultus, but the cultus as the type of what Christ himself fulfilled. 'The sacrificial transformation of Christ's body expressed in the flesh, the total obligation of his inner self accepted by God for the redemption of humanity – this was Christ's *teleiōsis*, the great achievement of his priesthood' (Sabourin 1973: 192). The author is out to contrast the limited and this-wordly nature of the sacrifice of the Aaronic priests and the covenant of Moses with the unlimited and cosmic nature of Christ's sacrifice and Christ's covenant. He is not aiming at a close and restrictive identification of Christ's work with the Day of Atonement, but at choosing certain Hebrew religious institutions to contrast them with their fulfilment in Christ. 'His theological estimate of Christ is that of the divine Son who has spoken the eschatological message of salvation, and the High Priest who has entered, not the earthly, but the heavenly sanctuary to make a lasting atonement for God's people' (Mosothoane 1974). As Mosothoane also states, the response of faith is also a very prominent theme in the epistle. It is necessary to get this clear in case Hebrews should be taken as the paradigm of how Christ's work must be identified as sacrificial and of what particular type of sacrifice Christ in fact offered.

'In the Jewish religion, in the time of Our Lord, the Day of Atonement, with its stress on sin and expiation, with its fasting and solemn rest and inactivity, was the supreme day of the year: yet it was but one day; within the year some twenty days of full festival joy also occurred, and some forty other days were observed as happy memorials of the works which God had wrought especially in relatively recent times, on behalf of his people' (Buchanan Gray 1925: 322). This then is one good reason for the author of Hebrews to have selected it for special treatment. Another good reason is that it culminated in the entry of the high priest into the holy of holies and was consequently the type fulfilled in Christ's victorious entry as the pioneer man into the Heavenly Holy of Holies. The picture therefore is that Christ has entered, has offered, not that there is a heavenly sacrifice going on still. The emphasis is on the achievement of Christ, the victory won. 'Hebrews nowhere states that Christ's sacrifice is either renewed, offered, re-presented or even prolonged in heaven. There, Christ's sacerdotal activity consists in being present and in interceding' (Sabourin 1973: 195). His prior act is that of having expiated, having entered. The Day of Atonement ritual is important to Hebrews because of what the author wants to say concerning the fulfilment of all priesthood by Christ and concerning the entry of Christ the high priest into the greater sanctuary. He goes in not only with the blood of expiation, but with *the blood of the covenant*.

In the crucial ninth chapter of Hebrews, the author sketches the cultus and holy place attached to the first covenant, including the 'place of expiation', into which the high priest enters once a year. He then turns to Christ, whose priesthood is superior, whose sanctuary is 'not made by men's hands', who takes with him his own infinitely more potent blood, who offers himself, 'a spiritual and eternal sacrifice' to cleanse from deadness, and who mediates a new covenant which is also a testament of the death of the old covenant which Moses had ratified in sprinkled blood. So either by confusion or fusion, Christ's blood is both the blood of expiation and that of covenant making. The author thus 'identifies in the death of Christ the sacrifice of the covenant in blood, achieving the redemption of the people and the renewing of the covenant on the Day of Atonement, which secures eternal redemption by the "redemption" (expiation) of sins. Sin being the breaking of the covenant, it is by restoring the Covenant in his blood that he achieves the redemption of the people by the expiation of sins' (Bourassa 1970: 165).

Spicq (1953) sees the message of Hebrews in terms of Christ offering his sacrifice as an effective act of covenant repair. By his emphasis on the 'blood of the eternal covenant' (Heb. 13.20) in his final punchline, the intention of the writer is far more than merely to extract an allegory from the Day of Atonement but to see Christ's blood as restoring and re-establishing the covenant between God and man. Christ fulfils both Moses and Aaron by conflating their roles: his blood effects both sacrifices. Manson brings these matters out clearly in his commentary also (Manson 1951). This covenant renewal stress in Hebrews is so often forgotten and it is assumed that the Epistle is taking sacrifice as an act of expiation pure and simple, whereas it is in fact a dual purpose sacrifice, cleansing and reconciling *and* making covenant. In another significant way too Christ is referred to as the liberator, deliberately evoking the language of the Exodus. He 'quite gratuitously frees us from slavery, so that we become "his own"' (Lyonnet & Sabourin 1970: 103).

It is as well to point out that Christ is both sacrificer and sacrificed, priest and offering. His *intercession* is essential to his expiatory ministry: in this he goes certainly beyond the role of the goat in the Day of Atonement rite and takes on the triumphant role of the high priest who has succeeded to the role of the king and has taken his own blood into the heavenly sanctuary and ever lives to make intercession. The culmination of the work of the Levitical priesthood was the Day of Atonement: so Christ performs his Day of Atonement. But this does not mean that the Day of Atonement culminated all sacrifice. It is not quite enough for Aulen (1931: 93) to say that Hebrews 'regards the sacrifice of Christ both as God's own act of sacrifice and as a sacrifice offered to God', when this particular sacrifice is singled out because of what it meant for priesthood, the sacrifice of Christ as compared to that of the Levites. Even in its most prominent function, the Levitical priesthood cannot accomplish what Melchizedek was, never mind what Christ is. *Christology*, not the cultus, is the theme of Hebrews. All the typology, including that of the heavenly sanctuary, traceable to Num. 8.4, Exod. 25.9 and 40 and certain intertestamental works, is devoted to this end. This would explain why certain crucial factors of the Day of Atonement ritual, such as the goat for Azazel, are just not pursued at all. The fact is that, even in the Epistle to the Hebrews, where sacrifice seems to loom so large, it is incidental to the theme.

It is possible to approach Hebrews from a different angle. If sacrifice is seen in terms of uniting and reconciling the community of God and man and man and man, a definition ascribed by Clooney (1985: 3–4) to certain Hindu theologians, then the sacrifice of Christ as described in Hebrews is the action expressing the reality of sacrifice. Then, 'Jesus expresses the highest relationship between God and community and community and God', as both participate in a sacred event.

The reason for this general omission of the theme of sacrifice from all New Testament writings, except Hebrews, where it demonstrably is incidental, is *not* because Christ's work was not seen as sacrifice, but precisely because it was so obvious that it was *the* sacrifice, that the point needed no labouring for Jews and was not given prominence in those works aimed at Gentiles or at Jews of the diaspora, because other language was required to communicate with those outside the sacrificial tradition of Israel.

It should be pointed out that, in Hebrews, where inevitably much expiatory language is used, here as in the Johannine corpus, it is God or God in Christ who carries out the expiation, who is the *hilasmos*, active for us, cleansing sin away, sent as such by God (Heb. 2.17; I John 2.2; 4.10.) Dodd (1935: 94–6) has shown conclusively that both Septuagint and New Testament Greek usage lead to this conclusion. About the use of the term in Rom. 3.21–26, he says, 'the rendering "propitiation" is therefore misleading, for it suggests the placating of an angry God, and although this would be in accord with pagan usage, it is foreign to biblical usage' (1932: 55). 'This Hellenistic Judaism, as represented by the Septuagint, does not regard the cultus as a means of pacifying the displeasure of Deity, but as a means of delivering man from sin, and it looks in the last resort to God himself to perform that deliverance, thus evolving a meaning of *hilaskesthai* strange to non-biblical Greek' (Dodd 1931: 359). Even more apposite to consideration of the Epistle to the Hebrews are Westcott's words 'The modern conception of Christ pleading in heaven His passion, "offering his blood", on behalf of men has no foundation in the Epistle to the Hebrews. His glorified humanity is the eternal pledge of the absolute efficacy of His accomplished work. He pleads, as earlier writers truly expressed the thought, by His Presence on His Father's throne' (1889: 230). To this Moule adds (1962: 90): 'Let it [the term "sacrifice"] be rid of all evil connotations of bribery or propitiation.' It would seem that Morris's (1955) spirited defence of propitiation is in fact more of a defence of the wrath of God and its being taken seriously, since having accepted propitiation, he goes on to condemn placation. To take a stand against the eroding of the idea and fact of God's wrath is certainly defensible, but to link this with propitiation is rather needless, unless the underlying motive is a defence of Calvin, warts and all. For Denney (1917: 160–61) to have written on one page 'In the New Testament age sacrifice among the Jews was really a survival', and on the next page, 'Propitiation is a word we cannot discard', seems to be a most peculiar combination of the radical with the conservative, involving all sorts of contradictions. Young's (1967: 281) summary of Athanasius's teaching is much more helpful: 'the sacrifice had to be offered by God himself in a process of self-reconciliation, and, if we may invent the term, self-propitiation.'

References in the Fathers to definite sacrifices in the context of the atonement are few and far between and continue to be so in much modern theology. There is of course an irony about this, since the original word in Hebrew which arrived in the English language as 'atonement', the word *kipper*, came from an exclusively sacrificial context, as has been seen. The *Epistle of Barnabas* and Justin continued with the Day of Atonement imagery, finding Christ as the *scapegoat*, bearing away sins. This is most odd exegesis, precisely because Christ did *not* escape. He is also identified with the red heifer. Theodoret carried the Day of Atonement ritual still further typologically, when he identified the slaughtered goat with Christ's humanity and the scapegoat with his divinity, because it did not suffer! But even more serious is (Ashby 1972: 68) the loss of the context of Hebrews by the fathers, leading them to ask the question never mentioned in the Epistle, 'To whom is the sacrifice offered?' and to answer it as Origen (*Comm. on Romans* 4.11, quoted in Young 1967: 246–7) did: 'To the prince of this world.' We begin to have the fatal concept of the Atonement as an aversion sacrifice offered to the devil. No wonder that Rivière commented that the Fathers' atonement theology was 'wanting in depth' (1909: 251).

Much more helpful is the *rite de passage* structure, as applied to Christ's expiation sacrifice. In this model, Christ as the scapegoat passes into the chaotic danger area of darkness, that of the crucifixion; of injustice, inasmuch as all right of law is effectively denied him; of locality, because he is crucified 'without a city wall'; of community because sentence is passed on him by the Roman commander, and he dies between two brigands; of the underworld, because he is put into a rock-tomb. Christ as the holy sacrifice, the physical link with the divine, goes into God's presence cleansing mankind with his own blood, to ratify and celebrate the covenant with mankind with the Creator in his own blood.

But why is the New Testament not more explicit in the use it makes of sacrifice and sacrificial terms? Marcus Barth has much valuable comment on this. The New Testament starts from the event of Christ's life seen as sacrifice, *the* sacrifice, so obviously so that it is hardly necessary to spell it out. 'The sacrifice of Christ shows in a unique way the necessity, cost and character of relationship between God and man' (1961: 51–3). How can this assertion be substantiated? We have at our disposal a fact of the utmost simplicity and significance which has been so often overlooked, though the New Testament does not overlook it. Again and again in the gospels it is plainly stated, so plainly that its significance stands out like the clue in an Agatha Christie that has been staring the reader in the face throughout the whole story. This plain fact is the Passover.

FIVE

THE PASSOVER – THE MISSING LINK

The origins of the Passover Feast in Israel are disputed. Only one factor is agreed upon by all, that it is very old indeed in Israel, if not also outside Israel. The word *pesach* tells us little. The Baal prophets '*pasach*-ed' round their altar (I Kings 18.26), but we do not know exactly what they did do and even whether what they did has much connection with the prehistory of the Passover. Dancing was not associated with the Hebrew Passover and the aetiology of Exodus 12 cannot easily be fed back into the Baal prophets' choreography, though many have suggested that they limped, as the Lord skipped over the Hebrews' dwellings in Egypt. Attempts have been made to link the Hebrew word with Akkadian and Egyptian cognates and arrive at the meaning 'to make smooth' or 'harvest', but these are highly dubious. Segal (1963) and Glasson (1958) link the word with the verb used in Isa. 31.5, where the Lord's attitude towards Jerusalem (the action of *pasach*) is compared to a bird 'hovering over' its young. Now unless Isaiah was ignorant of fairly basic bird behaviour, he would have known that no bird hovers over its young. Kestrels and other raptors hover over their prey and kites have a way of patrolling their nests, while eagles will stand over their nestlings with wings stretched out, but they do not hover over them. The translators of the New English Bible either were rather vague on their ornithology (the bustard of Isa. 34.11 suits its companion assortment of owls and ravens as well as an albatross with a family of goldfinches) or thought that Isaiah must have been. The *pasach* verb must refer to an attitude of protectiveness. It is quite possible that the Passover got its name because of the Lord's protection of Israel. However, as with *kipper*, the derivation of the word meant nothing to later Israelites – for them it had the specific meaning of a certain feast that they knew well and with which they had been taught to associate certain events and rites.

The most widely accepted theory of the origins of the Passover is that it was a nomadic feast, which the Hebrews already observed before they arrived in Egypt, and that this was the *chag*, the trek-feast, referred to in Exod. 5.1. Unleavened bread and bitter herbs would be desert fare and it took place at the Spring full moon, before Bedouin would begin their trek to fresh pastures. 'It is a sacrifice of nomad or semi-nomad shepherds, offered for the good of the flock in spring, when goats and sheep drop their young, and when the journey to the summer pastures is undertaken' (de Vaux 1964: 17; Haran 1972). The equation of Passover with a nomadic offering of the first-born by desert Bedouin dates back to Wellhausen (1885). It is arrived at partly by the juxtaposition with the death of the first-born in the adjacent account in Exodus and partly by assuming that the seasonal desert custom amongst early Arabs makes this likely. The blood smeared on the door-posts and lintel would indicate an aversion sacrifice to deal with desert djinns or with plagues. It should be added that the offering was not really a lamb in the Wordsworthian sense but in the butcher's sense – it was a sheep that had reached its first year: it had to be a male, and it could equally well be a goat. The Passover was a night celebration, held at the full moon before the Spring equinox (Gray 1925). The Feast of Unleavened Bread, usually referred to separately by the Hebrew texts though held at the same time as Passover, the Feast of *Matstsoth*, is thought to have been an agricultural feast fused with its neighbour by King Josiah (de Vaux 1964: 17).

Segal disagrees with this theory of a double origin and of a nomadic provenance. He points out that *matstsoth* were equally to be associated with nomads, being flat 'drop-scones', made without leaven, and that the whole point of the feast was to get rid of leaven, not to offer first fruits of any kind (1963). He would see both autumn and spring as beginnings to the year for different agricultural reasons and would accordingly find Passover to be a New Year Festival originally, involving a community meeting (a *Qahal*) and a ritual cleansing. This ritual cleansing, in the case of Tabernacles, reached the proportions of the Day of Atonement and eventually became detached and observed separately in the post-exilic period. He sees the special costume not as a survival of the nomadic trekking dress, but as a prophylactic dress and the hyssop as a similar sort of 'lightning conductor'. There is also a natural connection between the sacred first-born and first fruits and the first of the year, so that 'the first-born was accounted for and redeemed with yet greater care. Here lies the origin of the intimate link between the first-born and the *Pesah*. It is derived from the character of the *Pesah* as a New Year Festival.' (165) The bitter herbs, like the garlic in the Dracula stories, were a protection against evil and the roasting whole prevented the bits from being scattered, since they were holy. Hence, for Segal, *Pesah* and *Matstsoth* were always one festival, separated because of the association of the former with the Exodus. 'The *Pesah* is a *rite de passage* . . . . It marks the passing from the old year to the new year' (186f.).

Two prophetic sayings (Amos 5.25 and Jer. 7.22) pose a question. Were these two prophets including Passover in their assertion that there had been no sacrifice during the Wilderness period? Did they mean to contradict the Exodus tradition so flatly? Or were they thinking primarily of the Temple sacrificial system and pointing out that there had been a time before the Temple or any fixed shrine when Israel had had its values and priorities right? Or are these sayings glosses from the exilic period, designed to accustom the Hebrews to a religion without sacrifice or Temple, on the grounds that there had been a time when sacrifice had been equally out of the question? Whatever the answer to this conundrum might be, it is generally accepted that an early, if not ancient, origin for Passover must be proposed. Both Rowley (1963) and Kruse (1954) would see these two texts in terms of the 'dialectical negation' technique already noted in the prophets (see ch. 3).

First fruits, of all sacrifices, are most open to being seen as a kind of tribute to the landlord, 'the recognition of what is his own' (Rowley 1963: 78). Kaufmann (1961, also Pedersen 1940) sees them as the original *raison d'être* for the feast, as offerings to the moon god. Here again, Segal points out quite relevantly that firstlings are generally offered soon after they are born, not in one great crop once a year. In any case in Numbers and Deuteronomy the firstling ceremonies are dealt with quite separately from Passover. The *Pesach* regulations, in fact, make no reference to firstlings. As noted above, he would see the connection as one of Passover being a time of accounting for the first-born, not as the prime and original cause of the feast.

The 'waving' of the sheaf (a sort of procession to the altar of the sheaf and then its withdrawal) is generally seen as not original to Passover. Segal sees it as 'a rite of sympathetic magic to encourage the growth of the crops which were then in the green' (198), while Gray (1925) finds that what must have had a variable date, according to the end of the harvest, became attached to the main feast. Beer fits his festivals in with his literary criticism and has *Pesach* originating in a J source from the Southern Kingdom, *Matstsoth* with a Northern E origin and the sheaf as arriving with the Holiness strand (H) (Segal 1963).

Interesting though origins may be, our immediate purpose is to find out what those who offered and ate Passover during the Old Testament period proper thought they were doing and supremely what the Jews of Jesus' time thought they were doing at Passover time. By these times they were not nomads and had no thought of trekking to summer pastures. They may have thought in terms of a New Year, though mention of the New Year does not exactly crowd out the texts of the Torah. They may well have seen the year as a whole, sacrificial year. Yet all these considerations, as far as can be seen, were not obvious to them when they ate the Passover. Our task is to find out what the obvious layers were of this rich cake of a Passover feast, with so many elements, so many ceremonies and practices, such a wealth of drama, such promise of varied future.

The liturgical directions for the Passover are given in Exodus 12 and repeated with some variations in Deuteronomy 16. In each case the kernel of the rite is in fact a *zebach* sacrifice, quite unmistakably. The word is used of it in Exod. 34.25 and it is called *qorban* in Num. 9.7,13. Unusual features are the blood smeared on the doorposts and lintel (changed to its being poured at the foot of the altar in Deuteronomy) and the instruction that no bones should be broken. Deuteronomy adds a 'calf' (NEB) to the list of possible animals, which Segal (204ff.) considers a scribal error, and would appear to alter the recipe to boiling instead of braaing (i.e. roasting over an open fire). Here also Segal thinks that the word *bashal* should be translated to 'cook' as the original meaning in times before the boiling method was widely practised. In any case, Deuteronomy's main emphasis lies on where the Passover must be sacrificed, not how it must be done. The Deuteronomist is concerned to adapt the Passover to shrine worship. The blood must therefore be poured at the foot of the altar, and must be handled by a priest, who must choose the victim, while the dress regulations are abandoned. Later practice continued along the lines of Deuteronomy, but never succeeded in changing the essentially popular, community nature of the Passover feast. By Jesus' time the feast had two quite distinct aspects to it. The killing of the animal and the disposing of the holy parts were performed according to Temple procedures at the Temple alone. The eating of the meal remained a home affair, with a different sort of ceremony, even though it was treated as a *chag*, a trek feast and took place at Jerusalem, the city limits of Jerusalem being extended to accommodate the numbers of family parties from the provinces. Jubilees 49 omits the unleavened bread and bitter herbs, but does add wine and prescribe that it must be eaten in haste in the Temple courts. What really separates the Hebrew Passover from its origins, whatever those might have been, is what distinguishes all things Hebrew from all things Semitic. This is something which centralization of rites at Jerusalem by the Deuteronomic reform could not basically affect. It is expressed by von Rad thus, 'The interpretation in Exodus 12 and Deuteronomy 16.1ff., which connects it with the saving history, sees in its performance an actualization of Yahweh's redemptive action in history' (1962: 253). Passover is the sacrifice which deals with God's actions for and in Israel at the Sea of Reeds. It is a thoroughly historical sacrifice feast, not only a cyclical fertility rite. The bondage under Pharaoh, the crossing over, leaving Egypt, liberation from Egypt, escape, saving and ransoming motifs, all find their place in Passover. The Septuagint makes the artificial word play connecting suffering, *pathos*, and Passover, *pascha*, via the verb *paschein*, 'to suffer'. Passover became gradually a 'Kompendium der Heilsgeschichte' (Füglister 1963: 202). Brock-Utne finds in the origins of Passover a tribal covenant meal as well as a Spring Feast, and asks what could have been more suitable for the exit from Egypt (1934). In Israel we have the association of cult with historical event, with events seen and understood as having happened at a certain time and in a certain place. This probably began with Passover and continued into the other feasts until the whole sacrificial year was full of Yahweh's relationship with Israel through his actual deeds for them. Whatever its origins, Passover was the Festival of Deliverance from Egypt. Welch (1936) called the Passover a 'palimpsest' (a technical term used of manuscripts that have been erased imperfectly and then re-used). No wonder that, according to II Kings 23.21, Josiah ordered the Passover to be sacrificed to inaugurate his renewing of the covenant between Israel and Yahweh. 'The various different rites became, like the Passover, memorials of God's saving acts in Israel's history, and of the special covenantal relation which Yahweh had established with Israel. The Exodus from Egypt determined the content of the first fruits liturgy' (Young 1967: 73).

Segal, while identifying the Passover as a New Year Festival, with secondary connections with harvests, also emphasizes this historicization. The myth of creation is replaced by the creation of Israel. Füglister points out that the ancient canticle of Exod. 15.1–8 combines the two images of Yahweh conquering chaos and at the same time conquering the hosts of Pharaoh. Passover is another example of the structure of the *rite de passage*. Israel is brought from slavery to freedom, from death to life, from night to day, from an old to a new aeon. This 'holy danger' period is crossed then and in every subsequent year by sacrifice. Once again the point is not that there are or may be pre-Moses or pre-Hebrew sources for the liturgy of Passover. This is interesting but makes way for the real point, which is that Moses took a well-known sacrificial practice or set of sacrifices and stamped upon it the covenant relationship of Yahweh with Israel, in which Yahweh acted, a covenant was made and sealed and actualized in the blood of sacrifice. In this case, the sacrifice remained an essentially joyful and homely affair, a barbecue/braai, in which even Englishmen could take part without squeamishness.

Passover was a sacrifice in which blood was shed. As has been seen, the original purpose may well have been apotropaic, to ward off some threat, such as the slaying of the first-born. Rendtorff (1967) maintains that blood had originally no part in *'olah* or *zebach* sacrifices. In the case of the Passover an old apotropaic rite, when integrated into the Hebrew sacrificial system, took on the cleansing function of the *chattah*, as preliminary to the *pesach zebach*. 'So in Israel the old apotropaic rite would be generalized and, from a mere sign, the blood would become a vehicle of divine purification and life' (McCarthy 1969: 176). This is a very important point. Whether or not the original rite of smearing the doorposts and lintel with blood was a rite of propitiation, or of aversion, or should merely be called apotropaic, the later development of Passover left all this behind, and the pouring of the blood at the foot of the altar leaves the Passover as the sacrifice of all sacrifices where blood has an expiatory, cleansing function, and where expiation itself is the *first* movement in sacrifice, with the remaining movements to follow. 'Like all sacrificial blood, according to the view of the later books of the Old Testament and Judaism, the Passover blood had expiatory value. It could make expiation for those for whom the lamb was offered, that is, blot out sin in the genuine biblical sense' (Füglister: 355). This is borne out by the other cleansing ritual of Passover – the sweeping out of all old leaven.

This is a different sort of cleansing, almost an upside down *minchah*, but, if anything, an even more obvious rite of purification preparatory to the main sacrifice. Cleanse away the old; celebrate with the new.

In fact, in Passover we have a wonderful balance between expiation and covenant, for just as the Exodus is meaningless without Sinai, so also even the blood of Passover does not only have the quality of the blood of the purification ritual, but also that of Covenant. 'In the course of Israel's history, it gathered to itself more of covenant significance and came to be celebrated as the sacrifice which recalled the blood-bond made between Yahweh and his people and which sealed afresh their mutual relatedness through the common feast' (Dillistone 1955: 249). This covenant sealing ritual was perhaps over-emphasized by Trumbull (1887) and has consequently been under-emphasized since then. It should nevertheless be remembered that the covenant of Mount Sinai, translated later in terms of various recessions of Torah, was the basic relationship of Israel with God. As such, it was expressed in sacrifice, which in turn demonstrated Israel's obedience to God. This is why the prophets found it so ridiculous that anyone could offer sacrifice, which betokened obedience, and then flagrantly disobey. This sort of action made no sense at all. Better forget the sacrifice if they were not going to obey. Furthermore this obedience is *covenant obedience*, an obedience born of relationship, the relationship of the covenant: 'I am your God, you are my people.' When Christ's sacrifice is described as the 'sacrifice of obedience', it is this sort of obedience that is its meaning, the obedience unfulfilled by Israel, but fulfilled by Christ. It is also very significant that the Renewals of the Covenant described in II Kings 23.21–23, II Chron. 35.1–18; 30.1–27, and Wisdom 18.6–9, are inaugurated with a solemn Passover. Passover and Covenant are intimately connected, so that Passover is not only the Exodus feast, but also the Sinai feast, and the covenant is not only expressed in the Feast of Tabernacles, but also in the Passover.

There is a strange dearth of references to Passover in the prophetic literature, the Wisdom literature and in the Psalms. Apart from a rather dubious reference in Chronicles it would seem that Passover had fallen into desuetude until Josiah's reform. An even more radical suggestion would be that it had never been celebrated, as a liturgical act, until then. Be that as it may, it still remains an enigma that a feast which became so crucial to the Hebrews should need reviving.

At this point the links between the Exodus and the succeeding Passover should be investigated. In Exod. 12.14 Passover day is decreed to be a 'remembrance' (*zikkaron*). This word has been a fruitful cause of misunderstanding ever since. The verb *zakar* and its immediate derivatives are rarely used in Hebrew of a purely cerebral activity, as the English word remember is used. Nor is it used in the sense of a calendar commemoration, such as a commemorative stamp, which marks the birth of, say, Jane Austen 200 years ago and does no more than that. Nor, clearly, can the word *zakar* mean 'repeat': there are other Hebrew words to convey that particular meaning. De Vaux (1964: 24) brings out the meaning as regards Passover in his quotation from the Mishnah, 'Him who performed all these wonders upon *us* and upon our fathers, and who brought *us* from slavery into liberty', and in St Thomas's definition of 'a sign which simultaneously calls to mind the past cause, manifests its effect in us and announces the glory of the future' (*Summa Theologica* 3,qu.60 art. 3). When God 'remembers' Israel, he does something fairly dramatic about or to Israel. So also the Passover actualizes the past deliverance by Yahweh of Israel into the situation of the present Israel – 'all these wonders upon *us*'. Driver points out that the *azkarah* of the *minchah* offering has the meaning of a token, a part reserved and representing the whole. The word obviously shares the same root and is part of the *zakar* family. Again we have the linking action of sacrifice with something outside the sacrifice. It is a similar concept to the practice at Rome in the early days of the eucharistic liturgy of taking a portion of the consecrated bread, called the *fermentum*, and sending it to other congregations in the city as from the papal mass. The action is similar, but the Passover *zikkaron* is concerned with the link from one event to subsequent generations of Hebrews separated in time from that event. Marcus Barth combines the two ideas in his comment on Passover, 'This sacrifice is token and celebration of redemption given by God' (1961: 21). 'The Paschal Meal then was commemorative of past redemption, of the interposition of God at the beginning of Israel's history; and the chief constituents of the meal, – the Paschal victim, the unleavened cakes, the bitter herbs – were commemorative symbols whose meaning was expounded during the meal' (Gray 1925: 379).

With this in mind, borne out by the Passover liturgy, as Jeremias (1966) and others have shown, it is no wonder that the Passover attracted to itself a whole range of salvific acts of God throughout

Hebrew history and beyond. Barrosse (1968) has brought this out in a little known article. He points out that, in the Septuagint text of Jer. 38.8 (Hebrew 31.8), the new promised Exodus will also take place at Passover time. Also associated with Passover by attributed dating were the release of Joseph from prison, the anniversary of the creation of the world, the circumcision of Abraham, the sacrifice of Isaac, and the future coming of Moses and Elijah, the resurrection of the patriarchs and the end of the world. What needs to be taken very seriously is that by Jesus' time Passover was *the* celebration of salvation in Israel and had attracted to itself all the mighty works and acts of God known to the Hebrews. Vermes (1961: 211) has emphasized the close connection in Jewish theology of the attempted sacrifice of Isaac, the *aqedah*, with the expiation offering of all and any lambs in the Hebrew sacrificial round, while Spiegel (1967) claims to have discovered a haggadic tradition, present in Jewish thought before Christ, that preserved a legend that Isaac *was* slain by Abraham and rose from the dead. Be this as it may, *aqedah*, according to Jubilees 18.18/19 was associated with Passover as having taken place at the same time of year. With this incredibly rich set of associations of Passover with the creation, the myth of the victory over chaos and the whole future of the world, let alone with the *aqedah*, rescue of Israel from Egypt and the making of the covenant between God and his people, let us turn to a date in Jesus' life when he kept Passover, at Passover time.

Thanks to the monumental work of Jeremias (1966), there can be no doubt about the role played by the Passover in the life of the Jew of Jesus' day.

Despite the trek up to Jerusalem it must have been the feast of feasts because of its intimate nature, its participating liturgy, its mood of jubilation, its feasting. It had something of the quality of an old-style Christmas in Europe. Philo tells of the increase in the area of Jerusalem to allow space for parties coming in from all quarters to celebrate al fresco. He also says that the Passover was no longer restricted to adult males and to this the New Testament seems to add that women took part in some way. The Romans added to the occasion by releasing a prisoner. The Samaritans kept the feast 'old-style', with the dress, the haste and the blood-smearing prescribed in Exodus 12. The Falashas of Ethiopia, who may well have preserved the customs they left Israel with centuries ago, have only one sacrifice in their calendar – the Passover, celebrated publicly and preceded by a fast.

After the destruction of the Temple in AD 70, the killing and eating of the lamb disappeared from the rite, because it could no longer be slaughtered at the Temple and sacrifice was forbidden to be performed anywhere else. Passover became a vestige of a sacrifice, still to this day tremendously impressive. How much, much more so it must have been in its full glory and joy in Jesus' day.

What is striking about all four gospel accounts is the emphasis they lay on the *fact* of Passover, that it was then that certain events took place. Of the 31 explicit references to Passover in the New Testament 22 are concerned with the Passion narratives, and are almost equally spread over the four accounts (4 in Matthew, 5 in Mark, 6 in Luke and 7 in John). In addition, there is the identification of Christ as the paschal victim in I Cor. 5.7. It is generally accepted that John's schedule of the Passion makes Jesus' death to coincide with the slaughtering of the Passover lambs at the Temple, while the Resurrection takes place when the sheaf was being presented. The synoptics identify the Last Supper as a Passover meal, though the roast lamb is not mentioned. There is no need to trace the great controversy that still rages around the question of whether the synoptics were right in identifying the Last Supper as a Passover Meal, or whether the Johannine account is correct. It has always seemed a little odd that New Testament critics tend usually to support the historical accuracy of the synoptic accounts over against those of the fourth gospel, where there is a clash of any kind, but when it comes to the Last Supper a volte-face is accomplished and John's chronology becomes right. But the four accounts are so weighted with insistences that it was Passover time that there is no need to open the debate here. Box's (1909) argument about 'this Passover', the reference to the Last Supper in Luke 22.15/16; and Burkitt's contention (1916) that Mark got confused and thought that the Last Supper was a Passover, when he was only a boy at the time, are dubious in the extreme.

'When Jesus had finished this discourse, he said to his disciples, "You know that in two days' time it will be Passover, and the Son of Man is to be handed over for crucifixion"' (Matt. 26.1). 'It was before the Passover festival. Jesus knew that his hour had come and he must leave this world and go to the Father' (John 13.1). Now it has long since been the custom to drive a wedge between what Jesus might have said and what the gospel writers thought he said. This is much too complicated a matter to discuss here. But it does seem clear that the gospel writers (at least Matthew and John) were intending to convey that Jesus was aware of the significance of his impending death at Passover time – or at least that the gospel writers were aware of its significance. It did not escape their notice, to put it mildly, that it was Passover, though it has been escaping Christian thought ever since. Christ died and rose at Passover time. This was no accident. To argue that it was an accident is to run directly counter to biblical thought, which does not believe in accidents, and to lay every other event open to the charge of 'accident' all the way through. We cannot pick and choose our accidents. Either Jesus died at Passover time, by God's design, or he died by accident. We cannot have him dying by design, at Passover by accident. The evangelists will not have it so. 'In any case, at a very early date in the history of the church the Messiah's death was interpreted in terms of the soteriology of sacrifice, and in view of this great significance and the month of its occurrence, it is not surprising that it should have been thought of specifically as a paschal sacrifice' (Burkill 1956: 167). 'He connected His own death as closely as possible with the sacrificial cult, with the sacrifice of the Passover' (Brunner 1934: 479). According to the gospels, Christ died at Passover time and this was meant to be so.

'On the first day of Unleavened Bread the disciples came to ask Jesus, "Where would you like us to prepare your Passsover supper?" He answered, "Go to a certain man in the city, and tell him, 'The Master says, "My appointed time is near; I am to keep Passover with my disciples at your house."'" The disciples did as Jesus directed them and prepared for Passover' (Matt. 26.17–19, also in Mark 14.12–16; Luke 22.7–16). What was the purpose of the deliberate identifying by the synoptic gospel writers of the Last Supper with Passover? As far as can be seen they were not anticipating Oesterley (1925) and Jeremias (1966) and indulging in a debate over the dating of the events of the Passion. This particular issue was not a live one then and right down to this century few people questioned the synoptics' identification of Last Supper with Passover. Nor were the synoptic writers settling questions in either liturgy or in eucharistic theology. It has been a complaint of liturgiologists and theologians that there is so little evidence about the form of the Eucharist or its meaning from primary to secondary sources. It is almost as if, as with Hebrew sacrifices, the Christians just did Eucharist and asked no questions. It is ironic that the almost vestigial accounts of the Last Supper in the synoptic gospels have been thoroughly investigated from textual, contextual and subtextual points of view, all in order to clarify what they were never originally intended to clarify, the liturgy and doctrine of the Eucharist. What is often overlooked is that the Last Supper is seen by the synoptic writers as shedding light on *Jesus' Passion*, not on the Last Supper itself. There was no need in the early church to shed light on the Last Supper. They had been told to do it and they did it. The finer points of eucharistic dogma escaped them and the great eucharistic contentions which were to rend the Christian church had not been dreamed of then. But there was need to shed light on Jesus' death and resurrection, and what Jesus did the night before he died was of tremendous value, especially since it was believed that the Last Supper was instituted by Jesus as some sort of key to his death and to his resurrection. So his appointed time is near and he keeps Passover with his twelve disciples. Hebrews believed in appointed times, they kept Passover and there had been twelve tribes, no matter what subsequent higher criticism has done with them. It is therefore by no means extravagant to hold that the synoptic gospel writers believed that Jesus deliberately kept Passover that year in a way that showed that he saw himself as effecting what Passover effected – rescuing, liberating, renewing, re-creating, sacrificing, expiating, cleansing. In other words they believed he was saying, 'I am Passover, I am Moses, I am the God Liberator, I am Aaron, I am the Passover lamb.' The reason therefore why John does not describe the Last Supper is not because he knew nothing about it or was not interested in it; his purpose was no more to give liturgical directions or sacramental theology than was the purpose of the synoptic writers, but that he had another way of putting over what they said through their account of the Last Supper. John indicated clearly what Jesus was by his identification of Jesus' death with the slaying of the Passover lambs at the Temple. In a sense the debate concerning which of the two chronologies is accurate is irrelevant to the issue and it must be frustrating in the extreme for the gospel writers to have to endure a concerted policy in modern Christian scholarship of putting first what they put last and ignoring what they are at pains to put first. The real purpose of the narrative of the Last Supper is that it is the synoptics' attempt to show that Jesus is Passover, Liberator, covenant maker and sacrifice. 'The synoptic writers saw Jesus at the moment of the Last Supper as the royal, priestly and divine Messiah who shared with the heads of a new chosen people a meal that is at once the fulfilment of the Pasch and the beginning of the Kingdom' (Cooke 1960: 25).

'After singing the Passover Hymn, they went out to the Mount of Olives' (Matt. 26.30, also Mark 14.26). Again, the synoptics almost go out of their way to emphasize that it was Passover. This is just as important to them as the actual actions of the Last Supper itself. They finished Passover and immediately the events of the Passion, beginning with the agony and betrayal in Gethsemane, got under way. Hicks (1946) points out that the Passover Hallel included Psalm 118, which ends up with a description of a *chag*, a pilgrim feast in the context of Temple sacrifice.

'At the festival season it was the Governor's custom to release one prisoner chosen by the people' (Matt. 27.15, also Mark 15.6 and John 18.39). Doubtless there is an element of explanation of local custom here, though if this is the only reason, it is surely odd that, of all the four, Luke alone does not explain the incident. The point is made that it is at Passover that the Romans granted their token amnesty, and that, by common consent, it was not Jesus who was amnestied, but he was sent to his death. This was therefore a witting and willing choice of Israel at Passover time. They offered him, not to the Romans, for the political charge against him was manifestly false and did not even fool Pilate, but to Yahweh as their chosen Passover sacrifice.

'Now the Festival of Passover and Unleavened Bread was only two days off; and the chief priests and the doctors of the law were trying to devise some cunning plan to seize him and put him to death. "It must not be during the festival," they said, "or we should have rioting among the people"' (Mark 14.1–2; also Luke 22.1–2, where the festival is described as 'of Unleavened Bread, known as Passover'; John 11.55–57, where the feast is called 'The Jewish Passover' and where people coming up from the country for preliminary purification rites are looking for Jesus and wondering if he will be up for the festival). Several considerations emerge from these texts. First, the full title of the feast is sometimes used and Luke gives Unleavened Bread the priority as presumably being a non-technical term and then gives Passover as a Hebrew technical term, whereas they were two quite distinct aspects of the same feast or two conflated feasts. But the stress is on the impending Passover, that it should be clearly understood that it was Passover. Secondly, the Temple clergy wish to avoid the actual festal period for fear of rioting. In fact they did not succeed in avoiding this period and found themselves almost inexorably compelled to kill Jesus at Passover time, whether they wanted to or not. This, rather than just a taunt aimed at the night time arrest by the Hebrew Special Branch, may have been in Jesus' mind when he asked his captors why they did not arrest him in the Temple. It was forced upon them, and at Passover time.

There is this sense of the inexorability of it in all the gospels, not that Jesus is being swept along like a leaf down the rapids, as a good many modern Passion dramas, such as *Jesus Christ, Superstar* imply but that they, the Temple clergy, Pontius Pilate, Judas, found themselves compelled to do what they either did not want to do, or did not want to do at that time and in that way. Through it all sounds the refrain – *it was Passover*.

Thirdly the stress on Unleavened Bread is not to be ignored. The Unleavened Bread side of the feast was just as familiar to the Hebrews of Jesus' time and, with the destruction of the Temple in AD 70, was to become more and more familiar. Jeremias (1966: 61) has pointed out that the word of institution, 'This is my body' is modelled on 'This is the bread of affliction' in the Passover ritual. For 'structurally Jesus modelled his sayings upon the ritual of commenting at the Passover'. We now know about the different origins of Passover and Unleavened Bread, but to the Jew of Jesus' time they were but two aspects of the same feast of the Exodus. The connection of bread with bread of affliction is by no means fanciful. 'This is my body' identifies Jesus both with himself and with Unleavened Bread of the Exodus and 'This is my blood' identifies him with his own sacrifice which he is about to accomplish and with the sacrifice of the lamb at Passover. Once again the account of the Last Supper is not primarily a liturgical precedent for the use of English chalk-bread or sliver-wafers, but a statement of the Passover sacrifice Jesus is to be and to offer.

Whatever the Aramaic original of 'body' might have been, bread is the basic element of the Unleavened Bread festival and took the partakers straight back to the Exodus and the liberation from Egypt, while blood is the basic element in the Passover sacrifice and took them back to the same source. To the synoptic writers Jesus was saying, 'I am to be the new united Passover sacrifice, fulfilling all that is Passover.'

'Now on the first day of Unleavened Bread, when the Passover lambs were being slaughtered . . . prepare for your Passover supper?' (Mark 14.12, also Luke 22.7). John merely points out that at the end of the crucifixion it was the 'eve of Passover', which was, in fact, the time when the lambs were being slain at the Temple.

It is strange that commentaries often lay great stress on John's reference to Jesus' death at the very time when the Passover lambs were being slaughtered, though he does not make this specific, yet fail to comment on the synoptics' linking of the same event with the Last Supper. Yet once again there is the clear statement that both Last Supper and what Jesus is to accomplish have a great deal to do with Passover.

Once again also the purpose of the clear alignment of Last Supper with the slaying of the lambs is not to fix the liturgy of the Last Supper, which would have been sufficiently obvious to a Christian as close to the time of Jesus as the synoptics at least were, but to shed light upon what Christ was to do on the Cross. This is Passover time: they will eat their Passover: the lambs are previously immolated at the Temple by lines of priests and their blood is poured from basins at the foot of the altar.

Jesus holds Passover, or pre-Passover, at which he says, 'This is my body', 'This is my blood'. These words are not eucharistic definitive metaphysical statements taken from the writings of Aristotle or Plato, but the words of a young Jew at Passover time, when he has bread and wine in front of him, when he knows he is about to die on the following day. Again and again it is emphasized by the writers, for the benefit of all who can understand, that it is Passover time. This is Passover language, the language of sacrifice, and neither Jesus nor the gospel writers are concerned to produce eucharistic doctrine of the future, or statements for church synods, but an acted commentary on what is to follow. In other words the gospel writers, in their various ways, are putting over to their readers what they believe Jesus intended to say by his actions and words, quite simply, 'I, Jesus of Nazareth am the new Passover Lamb, the new bread, and tomorrow you will see the sacrifice accomplished.' In the case of St John the point is made in a different way. He is just as clear about the Passover time but sees the actual death as the demonstration of unity between the lambs and the Lamb. Christ the victim of the New Covenant is sacrificed on the Cross and the Last Supper eaten 'in the context of the Jewish Passover which has become our Holy Week . . . . The Passion of Christ and its "memorial", the Eucharist are not a continuation of the Old Testament Passover. They constitute a new Passover' (de Vaux 1964: 25–26).

But what of the Lamb? Apart from references to the actual Passover lamb the word is used in John 1.29 and 36 by John the Baptist, of Jesus, 'There is the Lamb of God; it is he who takes away the sin of the world.' Dodd (1953) has listed the various explanations given for the use of the term at Jesus' baptism. It has been suggested that Jesus is being called a sin offering. But the lamb was not the sin offering – this was either bulls or goats and in any case Jesus is not referred to as such anywhere else by John. A variant of this idea, still on the lines of a technical sacrificial term, is that Jesus is identified with the daily offering of a lamb in the Temple as an *'olah*. But this was not identified as a sin offering as such and it is doubtful whether the whole saying would have made sense in the context of baptism down by the Jordan. Unless a large amount of commentary and explanation has got lost, we must presume that the gospel writer, if not the Baptist, intended to speak fairly clearly to his audience and that people of his time would not have needed the sort of complicated footnotes provided with editions of the *Divine Comedy*.

Others have suggested that the intention is to refer to Jesus' innocence and gentleness under the character of the gentle lamb. This idea deserves short shrift. We are dealing with the Bible, not Margaret Tarrant. The animals that were slain at Jewish sacrifices were not babies, not was there the 'our dumb friends' type of sentiment abroad in Israel at the time. 'All interpretation of sacrifical ideas that lays stress on the innocence and frailty of the victim as represented by the young lamb is wide of the mark' (Gray 1925: 351). If it has not a sacrificial connotation it is difficult to see what it can refer to apart from Isaiah 53, to which we shall return later. Suffice it to say that both in Isaiah 53 and in Jer. 11.19, the image is that of a sheep led to the slaughter and, although the slaughtering would most likely be for the purpose of sacrifice, the image in both cases is concerned with the way a sheep is dragged to be killed, not with the purpose for which it is killed. The lamb became the image of uncomplaining innocence in Christian lore, because of a confusion with baby sheep, as is shown in the Austrian traditional poem from *Des Knaben Wunderhorn* (I, 304), used by Mahler in his Fourth Symphony:

> John lets the lamb go,
> And butcher Herod looks out for it!
> We lead a patient one,
> A blameless, patient one,
> A dear lamb to death!

A more frequent assertion is that the Baptist was referring to Isa. 53.7. To this has been added a philological argument, that the word *amnos*, a lamb, is, in John, a mistranslation of an original Aramaic word *talya'* which means a young man. This in turn is a reference to the servant of Isaiah 53. John, the evangelist, has mistakenly assumed that the word was the Hebrew word *talech*, which does mean a lamb (Bernard 1928). This is a case of misplaced reverence for an original Aramaic saying. Dodd (1953) has shown that the Septuagint never translates either *talech* by *amnos* or, where it occurs, *talya'* by *pais*. The whole identification rests on the assumption that those present at Jordan, or at least those who were to read the fourth gospel, would have picked up a reference to a lamb as a reference to the sheep and thence to the servant and thence to the sacrifice for sin offered by the servant four verses later. Now although we must reckon with some Jews knowing large sections of the Torah, and sometimes the Prophets, off by heart and being able to juggle around mentally to pick up allusions, the whole exercise is rather a complicated one for what would appear to be a fairly simple acclamation. In any case the Greek of Isa. 53 reads *probaton*, a *sheep*.

It is in fact an acclamation, not a literary allusion. Hence some including Dodd have seen the term as a messianic title in which the Messiah is at last seen as functioning as an expiation of sin. The Lamb of God is the King of Israel. Some quaint imagery has been added to this in the form of the 'bell-wether' image – Christ is the ram who leads the flock with his bell. This is really too much, since we are dealing with Palestine, not Wensleydale, or cowbells in Austria. In any case the creature is a lamb of some sort, not the pugnacious and seasoned old ram who leads his flock. But of course the theory does not depend on the ram and his bell.

A theory has recently been put forward (du Plessis 1987) that the Lamb, as used as a title in St John's Gospel, is a royal title, with no sacrificial meaning attached to it at all. No evidence is led to support this. It would be tempting to tie the title in with king-sacrifice theories, but this would not suit the author of the article, who wishes, as from the Reformed tradition, to get rid of all sacrificial references in case they lead to the Eucharist. He claims that there is no sacrificial language involved in the phrase, 'taking away the sins of the world'. This could be so if the words are taken in total isolation and at face value, yet how is sin taken away without sacrifice? It is another example of theological prejudices influencing scholarship.

At this point it would be as well to include in this study the various other references to lambs that might be relevant. In the Testament of Benjamin 3.8 there is a reference to a prophecy being fulfilled of the

Lamb of God and Saviour of the world, who will be handed over, though spotless, for the lawless and, though sinless, for the ungodly. He will be killed in the blood of the covenant for the salvation of the nations and for Israel and will confute Beliar and his aides. In the Testament of Joseph, one born of a virgin, in shining robes, of the tribe of Judah, will come as a spotless lamb accompanied by a lion at his left hand. He will save the nations and Israel and will inaugurate the kingdom (Hillyer 1967). These texts simply bristle with problems of all sorts and constitute very poor evidence for any reference to the Lamb, even in the Apocalypse. First, there are various textual problems, under which lies the serious doubt concerning the extent to which Christian additions, taken from the Apocalypse, may not have been added into this late Hebrew work. Secondly there is the question that applies to most intertestamental literature. Just to what extent did any given work have wide circulation, would its thought have percolated through to the sort of people who either formed the crowds addressed in the gospels, or who in turn might have read or heard the gospel themselves? We can assume that most Hebrews would be tolerably well acquainted at least with the Torah, if not the rest of the Palestinian 'canon' of the Old Testament. But how much familiarity can we assume in ordinary Jewish folk with, say, the Testament of Joseph, even if it was in the form we have of it now? Thirdly to what extent is there a flowing together of images to form the one image of the Messiah? Even assuming that the text of the Testament of Joseph is genuine, how certain is it that the lamb is the Messiah, rather than that Messiah *and* lamb have not coalesced into one composite figure. In Enoch, there is a horned lamb that champions Israel, but even if this unusual and somewhat bizarre figure had any effect on New Testament literature, does the lamb *originate* with the Messiah figure? Is there not a common source for all lambs? Lastly, even if the language of the Apocalypse owes anything to Jewish intertestamental literature in this respect, how much effect is it likely to have had on the Baptist, addressing his mixed crowd of people down by the Jordan?

In I Peter 1.19, the language is purely that of atonement. 'The price was paid in precious blood, as it were of a lamb without mark or blemish – the blood of Christ.' Although Messiah of course means 'Christ', there is no evidence of the sort of victorious Messiah suggested above. The language, like that of Paul, is in fact sacrificial, with an overlaid commercial or juridical interpretation, that of the price paid.

In Rev. 5.6, 'standing in the very middle of the throne, . . . a Lamb with the marks of slaughter upon him. He had seven horns and seven eyes, the eyes which are the seven spirits of God sent out over all the world.' He then receives power, is praised by the assembled throng and breaks the seals of the last acts. The saints are described as having washed their robes white 'in the blood of the Lamb' (Rev. 7.14). From then onwards the Lamb becomes a title for Christ. The Lamb is the bridegroom of the church and the Lamb is the light of the heavenly city. For many of these images we do not have to look much further than canonical Old Testament apocalyptic – Daniel and Zechariah. Obviously the Apocalypse has drawn heavily upon previous canonical or deuterocanonical apocalyptic. But where has the Lamb come from? In the Old Testament itself the Lamb is never a messianic figure as such. It may be that a few so-called intertestamental works bring the Lamb and the Messiah into conjunction. But the Lamb remains, though identified by Revelation with the Messiah, primarily a sacrificial figure. This is why he stands in the middle of the throne *as* (*hōs*) (not 'as if') slain, or 'with the marks of slaughter upon him' (NEB). The writer of the Apocalypse has identified the Lamb with the Messiah – up to now they have been quite different : from then on they are two roles of the one person, Jesus the Lamb and the Messiah. Van Unnik describes the Lamb of the Apocalypse as a slaughtered lamb with divine attributes (1970). It is surely this way round, not Messianism interpreted via Christ's suffering. John starts with his slain Lamb, who then becomes all-glorious. The Lamb of Revelation is the same Lamb as that of John 1.29, triumphantly acclaimed as the Messiah. The Lamb is, finally, the Passover lamb and none other, Jesus, slaughtered at Passover time, like the Passover lambs.

To the crowd at Jordan, to the readers of the fourth gospel and even to the readers of the Apocalypse the most obvious of all slain lambs was the Passover lamb. In this instance it is surely the obvious, the well-known, the readily recognized, the easily understood that counts, not the ingenious, the tortuous, the remote. Dodd identifies the Lamb of God with the King of Israel. A reply can be ventured that this is what it came to mean, but not then at that moment on the banks of the Jordan. What it then meant and always means, together with and side by side with the King of Israel, was the Passover Lamb, whose blood was poured at the altar-foot as a sin offering, whose feast, its various richnesses added to down the centuries, meant rescue, covenant, victory, care, creation and future glory for Israel and now was going to be operative, just as the blood was, for the world.

Dodd (1953) has also questioned the term *amnos* which, he says, is not used in the Septuagint to translate the Lamb of Passover. This word is used in John 1.29,36 and in Acts 8.32 (quoting Isaiah 53, the original of which, in the Septuagint, used the word *probaton*) and in I Peter 1.19, whereas *arnion* is used in the many references in the Apocalypse. On this subject an article by Chantraine is most revealing (1955). In it he points out that *arnion* is a diminutive of *arēn*, which was a general term in classical Greek and was often associated with sacrifice. The diminutive form is used only in Revelation and only of Christ. Elsewhere in Hellenistic Greek it is a general term for a young sheep. *Amnos* meant a lamb and was only used in sacrificial context. The Septuagint in fact uses the word *probaton* to translate the Hebrew *sheh* and, in Exod. 12.5, where it is specified that the animal may be either sheep or goat, the word *arēn* is used to indicate 'sheep'. The very fact that the word *probaton* is *not* used does not mean that the Septuagint reference to the Passover Lamb is being avoided. The words uttered by John the Baptist were in Aramaic or Hebrew in any case. The evangelist has deliberately avoided a neutral word for a sheep and has opted for a word which did have sacrificial connotations. The same has been done by the Apocalypse, only with a different word. In a way the New Testament writers are improving on the Septuagint by making quite clear that it is the Passover Lamb that they are identifying with Christ.

Jesus is revealed by the Spirit, to the Baptist, to all present or to himself as God's chosen Lamb, chosen to be the New Passover of cleansing from sin, of rescuing a much wider public than Israel. 'For the evangelist the primary significance of the term lay in a reference to the Paschal lamb, with which the lamb of Isa. 53, through the influence of the Christian Eucharist, had become fused' (Hooker 1959: 104). The second part of this statement might well be questioned, – concerning how the 'lamb' of Isaiah got entangled with the Christian Eucharist and then influenced the image of Christ the Lamb; nevertheless the first part should stand, that the primary significance of the Lamb of God is in the Passover lamb. 'In John, the Lord's Supper is not a Passover meal. It is antedated by twenty four hours, so that the connection with the Passover is not, as in the Synoptics, that the Lord's Supper was a Passover, but that Christ is the perfect Paschal victim, crucified simultaneously with the sacrifice of the lambs in the Temple' (Higgins 1952: 77). After describing the Passover as a transition rite, Médebielle goes on to say, 'The sin of Israel and of the world makes of Jesus the Passover lamb, an expiatory victim' (1970 col.223). 'The same Christ is, as Lamb of God, sacrifice and leader in one' (Füglister 1963: 126).

It is suggested that, in the light of Jesus himself and of the people he was addressing and of the audience for whom the evangelists were originally writing, that Lamb of God meant Passover Lamb, that the Last Supper was intended primarily to reinforce and act out this identification; and that subsequently Christians soon saw the link between Jesus the Passover Lamb and Jesus the Messiah in terms of putting these two images together into the composite image of the sacrifice-Messiah; they also soon saw that the question of a Passover Lamb, that itself was a suffering and dying human being, had in fact been solved for them in the vision of Isaiah 53 of which they alone understood the inner meaning. But first and foremost the Lamb is the lamb of Passover.

The connection in the later Passover usage between the Passover lamb and the *aqedah* has already been alluded to. It remains to enlarge upon this further. *Aqedah* is already translated as meaning 'the Binding'. However, the verb is only found once in the Old Testament (in Gen. 22), apart from an adjectival form meaning, presumably, 'striped' and used in connection with the cattle that Jacob won from Laban. The Septuagint uses the verb *sumpodizo* 'tie the feet together', a very natural word to use of immobilizing sheep. Vermes and Levi, in articles incorporated into Yassif's volume on *The Sacrifice of Isaac* (1984), have traced the use of the *aqedah* theme in Judaism. Both are certain that the emphasis on the value of Isaac's attempted sacrifice does not come either from Christian influence or in reaction to Christian apologetic. Vermes demonstrated that the Targum on the subject (Neofiti) has Isaac as a *willing* volunteer for sacrifice (not a passive victim as he appears in Gen. 22). Also his sacrifice is to avail for subsequent generations of Abraham's descendants. Further, 'it would seem safe to assume that the Targumic Haggadah on the *aqedah* resulted from an association of Gen. 22 with Isa. 53, as a result of reflection on *martyrdom*. Hence in Isaac sacrifice and suffering were already united to play a salvific role for Israel to come. The liturgy of the Rosh Hashshanah contains a prayer that the sacrifice of Isaac will avail to avert God's anger from the present generation of His people.

The Mechilta of Rabbi Ishmael (second century AD) says that when God sees the Passover blood, he sees the 'blood' of the Binding of Isaac. We have therefore, within the Jewish tradition a nexus of the *aqedah* with martyrdom and sacrifice.

Abraham's obedience and the intended sacrifice of the innocent Isaac proved a ready challenge for patristic typological exegesis. The Targums had already referred to Isaac as the lamb (*amnos*) of God. Richardson's (1958:180) contention that the words said over Jesus at his baptism in the Jordan, 'You are my beloved son, in whom I am well pleased' (Mark 1.11; Luke 3.22; Matt. 2.17) are a conflation of Gen. 22 and Isa. 53, Isaac and the servant, has received unexpected support from Vermes for these reasons. The primary connotation must have been Passover and the secondary link with Isaac and the servant in the synoptic gospels, to which both Richardson and Vermes would add John 1.29 and 3.16. Theodoret of Cyrrhus is one of many patristic commentators to explore the typology Isaac–Jesus (Ashby 1972). Isaac is the type of the divine nature of Christ (*theotēs*), while the ram is the type of the human nature (*anthrōpotēs*). J. R. Brown (1938), drawing upon the fresco of the Isaac incident in the synagogue at Dura-Europos, suggests that Jesus saw himself as Isaac. The typology was also taken up by Irenaeus, the *Epistle of Barnabas*, Ephrem, Tertullian, Augustine, Isidore, Bede and Rabanus Maurus, even to the extent of seeing the wood of the Cross as the type prefigured in the wood carried by Isaac.

The Roman rite uses, in its canon, the most ancient part of the liturgy, Abraham's sacrifice of Isaac as an example of spotless victim and as a type of Christ's sacrifice and of the Mass. In Eastern Christendom the offering of Isaac in iconography stands for the relationship within and emanating from the Trinity (e.g. the famous Rublev icon). Of course this does not in any way prove that either Jesus saw himself as Isaac, or that the bystanders at his baptism, or the readers of the gospel, or John the Baptist, or even the evangelist, saw in Jesus' actions the *aqedah*. To suggest this would be to fall into the trap of going for the non-obvious. All that is suggested is that the early Christian writers might have reached the Christ-Isaac typology by means of the Lamb of Passover and its link at the feast with the *aqedah*. Hence they could say 'Jesus is Isaac, the lamb, by whom the sins of men are taken away' (Lyonnet & Sabourin 1970: 266).

'He said to them, "How I have longed to eat this Passover with you before my death! For I tell you, never again shall I eat it until the time when it finds its fulfilment in the Kingdom of God"' (Luke 22.14–16).

It is to be noted that this is from Luke's gospel, generally considered at least in many respects as having been written by a Gentile for Gentiles. Jesus stresses, again in the course of the Last Supper, two things. First, he has longed to eat this Passover with them before his death. Why? Is it because he had longed to set in train the Christian Eucharist? He could have done that at any meal together after he had selected his disciples. Is it because he wanted to have a last celebration with them? There is of course some element of 'last celebration' about it, but far more than that. Is it surely not because *this* Passover is the one before his death and he has been longing to show his death to them, his approaching death in the liturgy and language of this Passover (for Luke it *is* a Passover meal). Even for Luke this Passover is highly significant: it is before his death. Vincent Taylor (in commenting on this passage), admits that 'Paschal associations filled the mind of Jesus at the Supper' (1933: 183) and that the fellowship of the Last Supper was more intense as death was nearer. Secondly there is the eschatological statement, that he will not again eat Passover until its fulfilment in the Kingdom of God. Now does Jesus merely mean that he won't have another meal with them because he is going to die the following day? Apart from the question of whether he actually ate the fish on the shore of Galilee after his resurrection, his remark must have more meaning to it than that this was his last meal before they all met again in heaven. It is the Passover meal he is referring to, as Luke has pointedly demonstrated. The Passover, as has been seen, had gathered to itself a whole eschatology of fulfilment and of God's kingdom.

As Strobel points out, the language of Luke is very much in line with Passover eschatology (1958). Jesus eats this Passover with them, the *twelve*, before his death. The Passover is about to find its fulfilment in the Kingdom of God, for Passover brings fulfilment. No wonder then that Spicq identifies the heavenly sacrifice of Hebrews as the Passover. 'The heavenly sacrifice is the true '*sacrifice de passage*', *zebach pesach* (Exod. 12.2,7), the permanent Passover' (1953: 127). This is a highly significant identification, since, if this is so, it shows that all expiation has been performed by Christ, as Hebrews points out very clearly. There is now no more expiation, no more cleansing. But there is still sacrifice, the celebration of Passover, liberation accomplished, Red Sea crossed, kingdom come, blood shed, present praise and future glory.

'Six days before the Passover festival Jesus came to Bethany, where Lazarus lived whom he had raised from the dead. There a supper was given in his honour . . .' (John 12.1–2). What is certain about this text is the deliberate reference to the approaching feast. John wants his readers to make no mistake about the time of year and gives a six day warning by dating a previous event. What of course cannot be pressed is the possibility of other levels of significance. At Bethany Lazarus died and was raised: on this occasion, according to the fourth gospel, there is another meal at which Jesus is anointed against his burial. These events are obviously significant for John, since he picks them out vividly. It could well be that the reference to the coming Passover and to Lazarus, 'whom he had raised from the dead', when it is already quite clear from the previous chapter that Jesus has raised that Lazarus (and no other Lazarus is mentioned) and that it is Passover time (11. 45,55), is intended to take us from one act of liberation to the Passover act itself.

'The next day the great body of pilgrims who had come to the Festival . . . shouted "Hosanna" . . .' (John 12.12). Again, it might not be too fanciful to see that John is reminding his readers, through the fact of the peaceful and triumphant entry into Jerusalem, that this messianic acclamation happened at Passover time. This is the sort of fact that gave rise to the belief afterwards in Revelation that Jesus is both Lamb and Christ, sacrifice and saviour, at Passover time.

'Among those who went up to worship at the festival were some Greeks' (John 12.20). They are introduced to Jesus who tells them that the hour has come for the Son of Man to be glorified and that a grain of wheat must die before harvest comes. It is generally agreed that 'Greeks' must mean Jews of the Diaspora – Greek-speaking Jews. These people did made the trek to Jerusalem for the major festivals from time to time, especially for Passover, so that there must have been many such people who had experienced Temple sacrifice at Jerusalem, particularly the Passover. But could it also be that John deliberately used the term 'Greeks' to indicate the universal nature of this Passover event, for Jesus goes on to explain to these Greeks that he is to die and rise again. Now of course there remains the problem of Jesus' predictions of his passion, but the point is that John puts this prediction in this setting, of 'Greeks' coming up for Passover, at which Jesus was to 'fall into the ground and die', but bear a rich harvest.

'The Jews themselves stayed outside the headquarters to avoid defilement, so that they could eat the Passover meal' (John 18.28). The references to Passover, in this case at Jesus' trial, are purposeful and must indicate more than a topographical note to show the positions of Pilate, Jesus and the Jewish leaders on and off stage. There is surely some note of irony that the old Passover sees itself as defiled by the new and perfect Passover.

'Because it was the eve of Passover, the Jews were anxious that the bodies should not remain on the cross for the coming Sabbath, since that Sabbath was a day of great solemnity . . . so they did not break his legs . . . in fulfilment of the text of Scriptures: "No bone of his shall be broken." And another text says, "They shall look on him whom they pierced"' (John 19. 32–37). Again the writer of the fourth gospel takes great pains to emphasize the date and the feast. More important is the pointed identification of the unusual event of a crucifixion without the breaking of the fibula to hasten death, and the Passover prescription that the lamb must be whole. Both are unusual happenings: it was not often that prisoners died while they could still press upwards with their legs, and it was not often that sheep were roasted whole. The meaning is clear: for John, or for the fourth evangelist, Jesus was the Passover lamb of a new Passover sacrifice. It is perhaps significant that the fourth gospel, which does not draw directly on the Last Supper to illuminate the meaning of Christ's death, does seize on a variety of other Passover allusions to make the same point.

'During supper he took bread, and having said the blessing he broke it and gave it to them, with the words: "Take this; this is my body." Then he took a cup, and having offered thanks to God he gave it to them; and they all drank from it. And he said, "This is my blood, the blood of the covenant, shed for many. I tell you this: never again shall I drink from the fruit of the vine until that day when I drink it new in the kingdom of God"' (Mark 14. 22–25). In this instance some sort of decision has to be reached about the text. In default of a better solution, we should adopt the text of the New English Bible and accept for the time being that, in default of overwhelming evidence to the contrary, Mark wants us to believe that what was said at the Last Supper was actually said then and that the expressions used carry the normal meaning that would be ascribed to them *then*. We may perhaps also deduce that, since no sense of shock was registered on this occasion at the words 'This is my body, . . . this is my blood' we must look for some explanation of these highly provoking words that would not jar the normal religious sensibilities of a Jew of the time. Now cannibalism would most certainly be shocking to the disciples, while some sort of identification by substance and accidents would be utterly meaningless and right outside their comprehension. The only possible meaning that can be attached, it is submitted, is a sacrificial one. *NOT* that Jesus (and here is where the mistake has traditionally been made) was primarily concerned to identify the Last Supper as a sacrifice, but that the very actions of the Last Supper were a commentary on his own Sacrifice which was to follow (or at least, this was the way Mark saw it). He was saying to them 'Watch what I do and do it yourselves in the future: it shows me as your sacrifice, this is what my death is all about: I (and you in days to come) am showing forth my death till I come.'

The whole action is enclosed in Passover by Mark, beginning with the slaughtering of the Passover lambs and ending with Passover Hallel. What is also of decisive importance is the phrase 'the blood of the covenant', particularly when it is followed by the eschatology of drinking it new in the kingdom of God. Paul amplifies the covenant in his account of the Last Supper with, '"This cup is the new covenant sealed by my blood. Whenever you drink it, do this as a memorial of me." For every time you eat this bread and drink this cup, you proclaim the death of the Lord, until he comes' (I Cor. 11.23–26). In Paul in this passage there is no overt reference to Passover, but there is a very careful insistence on the new covenant, on 'the night of his arrest' and on the memorial *anamnesis*. Even in St Paul, the Last Supper points to Christ's death and afterwards proclaims it. Now St Paul's emphasis on Christ's Resurrection in so many other places makes the repeated proclamation of Christ's death an unusual comment on any Christian rite. Why Christ's death alone, with no Resurrection coupled with it? Surely the context of the first occasion of the Last Supper, at Passover or at Passover time, makes the reference to the proclamation of Christ's *death* natural even when set beside a kerygma which tended to start from Christ's *Resurrection*? The Last Supper is concerned with sacrifice, and sacrifice in this case, and in the case of the Passover, involves death. Hence the Last Supper does proclaim Christ's death, because it proclaims his sacrifice as the Passover lamb. The Resurrection, at that stage with which Paul is concerned, belongs to the future. But to return to the covenant. Jesus saw his blood as covenant blood and Mark is seeing the Last Supper as Jesus seeing his blood as covenant blood – the blood to be shed on the morrow and the covenant to be made anew then. That new covenant will have its own covenant renewal rite – the Last Supper. The nature of the Passover as covenant festival has already been seen. This is not a case of making the Passover bear a load that it was unfitted for, but a reminding of ourselves that there are several instances of the covenant being renewed in Hebrew history with a solemn Passover and of the content of the Passover liturgy itself. Passover, particularly for those outside Jerusalem, meant Sinai as well as Exodus. Petuchowski points out that *eis anamnesin* is a rendering of *lezakar* of the Passover Haggadah. Hence Paul may well have been the agent of the identification of Passover with Eucharist. It is 'a justifiable assumption that I Corinthians was written before the Passover season and it is natural that the Passover ritual should be in the forefront of Paul's thought' (1957: 293, quoting Davies 1948: 250). Even the blood of Christ is not only expiatory but also the blood of covenant sacrifice, as could not be more clearly indicated that by Mark's and Paul's accounts of the Last Supper (Füglister 1963). 'The relationship between the old covenant and the new, between promises and fulfilment, are brightly illuminated, if Jesus' last meal was a Passover meal . . . the Last Supper would still be surrounded by the atmosphere of the Passover even if it should have occurred on the evening before the feast' (Jeremias 1966: 88). 'Christ, as God, makes the covenant with mankind through the mediation of His own human nature; Christ, as man and as the priest who is vicar for mankind, makes the covenant with His father' (Cooke 1969: 32). Cooke goes on to claim that covenant, through Passover, dominates the thought of the synoptic gospels, even though the actual word is only used in the text of the liturgy of the Lord's Supper. This is probably too sweeping a statement, but covenant and covenant renewal is there in the gospel stories, both in direct allusions, like the Mount of Transfiguration, and through the Passover and the twelve disciples who are the twelve tribes of the new covenant – and the Last Supper was the last occasion when they were all together. 'No blood could seal a covenant, but blood of sacrifice; it was with such blood that the old covenant had become sealed' (Farrer 1968: 26). All this is alluded to in the famous statement of the Epistle to the Hebrews, that Christ is constituted shepherd by the blood of the eternal covenant (Heb. 13.20). Covenant theology is also found in II Cor. 3.6 and 14; Gal.4.24 and, above all in Heb. 9. It is, however, in the narratives of the Last Supper that covenant and Passover are set together and fulfilled in Christ's blood. There is an element of reconciliation about all covenant making. Long ago Curtiss pointed out the relevance of the lamb of reconciliation in Semitic sacrifices, 'the lamb makes peace and removes the enmity' (1902) being strikingly parallelled in Eph. 2. 13–17, where the blood of Christ brings peace. It is in covenant sacrifice where expiation and reconciliation meet.

'It was near the time of Passover, the great Jewish Festival' (John 6.4). Gärtner (1959) has pointed out the various links between John's version of the feeding of the five thousand and Passover. First there is the emphatic dating, 'near the time of Passover'. Then there is the question and answer dialogue, 'Where are we to buy bread . . .?', similar to the Passover Haggadah. Fish was evidently used as a substitute for lamb outside Jerusalem. There is the post-resurrection episode on the seashore of John 21. From Melito of Sardis up to present times the feeding of the five thousand has been taken as a prefiguration of the Eucharist. It could well be that, once again, it was not the Eucharist that the writer had in mind, but the *Passover* and what was to happen at Passover. This would particularly apply to John. The fourth gospel does not omit a Last Supper narrative because the feeding of the five thousand is a substitute. This is much too tortuous a solution. The references in the story of John 6 are not to the Eucharist but to the Passover meal. This is why, again in the fourth gospel, so many references are made by Jesus to himself as the bread of eternal life. A Jew would already understand that the Passover was not just a hearty meal, but the action of God made relevant through sacrifice. This is John's way of saying that Jesus is the action of God made relevant through sacrifice.

'The price was paid in precious blood, as it were of a lamb without mark or blemish' (I Peter 1.19). There is no phrase in Isa. 53 to suggest in any way directly a lamb without blemish. This is another instance where we must go for what was obvious to those for whom the words were written rather than for a complicated literary allusion after the style of T. S. Eliot. Jews knew that their Passover lamb must not be an 'export reject' – one-eyed, or diseased or lame, but a whole specimen. It was in the Passover regulations and they must have considered this every year. Selwyn traces this to midrashic exegesis of Leviticus 17–26 and Numbers 28–29 (Hooker 1959). Naturally in the sacrificial legislation an animal that was sound in wind and limb was indicated and Jesus was far more than that. But we do not have to go fossicking around in Isa. 53 to prove that. That was just the point that Peter was making – in Jesus we have a far more perfect sacrifice for our Passover, *the* spotless lamb.

'For indeed our Passover has begun; the sacrifice is offered – Christ himself. So we who observe the festival must not use the old leaven, the leaven of corruption and wickedness, but only the unleavened bread which is sincerity and truth' (I Cor. 5. 7–8). This is the only direct reference by Paul to Christ as the Passover sacrifice, but is clear enough to satisfy. There is no escaping his meaning. What is very interesting is that the unleavened bread is brought into the picture too. For whatever might have been the original separation between Passover and first-born offerings and first fruits, by Jesus' time all these themes had become woven into the Passover liturgy, including the new bread and the waving of the sheaf. This passage provides a clear link with the title often given to Christ by Paul of the *aparche*, the first fruits, which is also not only a technical sacrificial term, but again one intimately connected with Passover celebration.

The more it is realized what a '*Kompendium der Heilsgeschichte*' the Passover was in Jesus' time, the less do we have to look beyond Passover for the meaning of Christ's death in sacrificial terms. We have seen the reasons why Hebrews chose the Day of Atonement, and good reasons they were too, but the fact remains that the point of reference for the gospel writers was Passover. Surely also, the repeated insistence by the evangelists that 'it all happened at Passover' is *some* indication that Jesus too saw himself as fulfilling Passover. There must be some limit to the much vaunted gap between what the evangelists thought Jesus meant and what he actually meant.

In the sub-apostolic age and in the patristic period, the tendency is to ally Passover with Easter and to use all the symbolism of the Passover in the liturgy of Easter. The Roman-Gallican rite has this very strong tendency, as do the hymns of St John of Damascus. Christ as Saviour, Christ as Passover is the message, and since the liturgical year tended at this period to radiate from *Easter*, the dominant theme is that of 'Christ our Passover'. This has been overlooked in studies in the dogmatics of the patristic age. Theologians always tend to lead each other on in controversies and crusades against heresies, when the normal liturgical practice of the worshipping church continues to proclaim what the theologians are, in their preoccupations, not proclaiming. Easter was the Resurrection day, when Christ's triumphant work is proclaimed. It is his Passover, in which he is the lamb. So much so that the very word Passover is the Christian word for the feast of the Resurrection in all but a few European languages, of which English, unfortunately, is one. 'This Passover is our Saviour and our refuge' (Justin, *Dialogue* 72.1). 'They saw the sending of Christ, like the institution of the feast, as a gift of God to men who were in slavery to sin, death and the devil, the sacrificed lamb as a God-given means of redemption from this enslavement, and the blood of the lamb as the means of averting the evil powers of destruction' (Young 1967: 208). The sermons of Melito of Sardis lay great stress on the Passover as fulfilled in Christ. The lamb of Exodus-Passover is the type of Christ (Bonner 1940). Now this is in fact the use of typology, so whether much stress should be placed on this particular type when there are so many that are used by the fathers, is doubtful. However, much stress has also been laid on Melito as the extant example of Quartodeciman writing, and it is asserted that the Quartodecimans stand for the earliest and most genuine Passover tradition (Lohse 1953). Melito certainly took up the themes of Jewish Passover, including that of Creation (the Jewish legend that Creation had taken place on the date of Passover has already been alluded to) in his homily. His motive may well have been to emphasize the continuity, even to the extent of the actual date, from Hebrew Passover to Christian Pasch. The very insistence of the Quartodecimans on this variable day of the week, was not an obsession with dates, or anti-Jewish polemic ('we do it too, and on the same day'), but a sincere desire to proclaim Christ as the Passover sacrifice, vindicated as such by the Resurrection. What led Soter to move the Roman church into the fixed Sunday position for Easter, was not that he did not see Christ as Passover, but that he saw Christ so clearly as Passover that there was no need to insist in the confusing variable day or to follow the Jews so slavishly (Hall 1975). Liturgy and calendar proclaim clearly what the dogmatic writings are not so insistent about, that Easter is Passover. This could only meant that Christ is our Passover sacrifice. Now it may be that, because by this time the lambs were no longer slain at the Temple after AD 70, Passover did not for the Christians of this period present an image of animal sacrifice. This might be a reason why the liturgy shows no embarrassment about it. This means that Christians kept the imagery of Passover without experiencing the sacrificial rite itself. But by contrast it is equally true to maintain that the evangelists did know what happened at Passover and made it quite clear that Christ acted purposefully at Passover time. In any case it might be as well to see that early Christians lived in the joy of Passover celebration assured by the Resurrection, rather than in gloomy anticipation of the Cross.

Aphraates, in the fourth century, claimed that Jesus is the Passover lamb and that the Jewish Passover has now become 'illegal' (Neusner 1971: 36).

It should also be pointed out that, in Hebrew religion, sacrifice and suffering are *not* natural concomitants. Nobody would have considered that animals suffered when being immolated any more than they would consider the abattoir in terms of suffering. This is a mistake so easily and readily made – the equation of suffering and sacrifice. Their equation in the person of Christ was precisely because it was in the person of Christ. He was a most unusual sacrifice. Hence it was relatively easy to see that he suffered. But it was no easier to put sacrifice and suffering together in the person of Christ than it was to put Messiah and suffering. The two concepts are married in Christ. It is by no means certain that Isa 53, despite its references to the servant as a sacrifice for sins, gave rise before Christ to a suffering sacrificial servant idea. What little evidence there is seems to point to an identification of the servant with Israel, who by her exile would both suffer and be a sacrifice in some half-perceived way. But the idea of 'suffering because sacrifice' is not relevant at all to the period. *We* see suffering and sacrifice as one idea, because Christ combined them both and we are post-Christian. They did not see it that way, not even fully in the New Testament, where even in the Apocalypse the Lamb as slain and the sufferer are beginning to merge.

'The reality in this sacrifice is his obedience to the will of the heavenly Father and his love poured out in full solidarity with those who live in bondage under the destructive powers of sin and death' (Aulen 1931: 121). The obedience of Christ is often singled out as the new form of sacrifice undertaken by him. This removes the need to consider blood. Now there is no denying that Christ was obedient to the will of his father – that is what Gethsemane was all about. Nor is there any denying that beyond the New Testament, in early Christian times, there was a tendency to 'spiritualize' the nature of even Christ's sacrifice, just as in Western theology it has been called 'moral', 'ethical', 'spiritual', 'obedient' – anything to escape the crude realities of blood. But did Christ see it that way? Did the gospels see it that way? Did Paul see it that way? We have for some time been in the habit of imposing modern Western ideas of ethics on biblical ideas, and obedience is one of them. In Victorian England obedience to one's parents, regard for one's mother, obedience to one's officers, were sterling qualities, admired by all and manipulated by some. That finest of all nineteenth-century institutions, the Habsburg Empire, thrived on obedience. But obedience in the Hebrew world of Jesus' time meant obedience to God under the covenant, shown forth in following the Torah and in sacrifice. Temple and Synagogue were the visible expressions of this sort of obedience and both were supremely demonstrated in Christ. He fulfilled the Torah, in spirit, not in letter.

He fulfilled sacrifice by being sacrificed. He was obedient unto death, the death of the cross. He was not just obedient, but obedient unto the death of the cross. Likewise his sacrifice was not a sacrifice consisting of obedience, and nothing else – this is where the Hebrew construct case comes ambiguously into English. His sacrifice was sacrifice unto blood done in obedience. Of course in this respect, obedience is a new element in the offering – it does not apply to the animal or to the cereal, which does not know whether it is being obedient or not. Obedience, covenant obedience, now becomes an element in the offering as well as in the offerer.

Sacrifice is communication between man and God and God and man through the medium of material things which form part of the life of man. Jesus' life was the supreme act of communication between God and man in which God took the initiative and man responded in the material most familiar of all to him – the actual human person. This sacrifice set deliberately at Passover time comprised within itself all the traditional sacrificial motives which had already clustered around the Jewish Passover, from creation, through expiation, reconciliation to covenant remaking and promise of future blessing. Into it was poured all the response to God that humankind is capable of – ethical, moral, spiritual. But it was first and foremost the supreme act of sacrifice performed between God and man and man and God, and through this strong bond of the blood of Christ man's assurance has been flowing ever since. Christ our Passover is sacrificed for us, therefore let us keep the feast.

'The myths of Christ's sacrifice and of his victory answer to empirical realities within the historical community which for historical reasons, if for no other, can be designated and symbolized in no other way. Such myths belong to the very existence of the historical church and whatever validity and worth are ascribed to the church itself can be ascribed to them' (Knox 1959: 179).

'Jesus did not condemn sacrifice; indeed, he offered himself as a sacrifice; he is the paschal victim and his sacrifice is the sacrifice of the New Covenant. This is the perfect sacrifice, by reason of the nature and disposition of the victim; he offered himself of his own free will, in an act of obedience. It was perfect also by reason of the manner in which it was performed; it was a total gift, in which the victim returned wholly to God; a communion sacrifice more intimate than man could ever have suspected; an expiation-sacrifice sufficient to atone for all the sins of the world and precisely because it was a perfect sacrifice which at one stroke exhausted all the possible aspects of sacrifice, it is unique' (de Vaux 1961: 456).

SIX

SACRIFICE AND
THE EUCHARIST

If we are to understand any act of sacrifice, there are two factors that must each time lead the understanding. First, there is the general understanding of sacrifice, not in terms of motives and purposes that only explain some sacrifices, but as the language of communication used from time immemorial by men when they have approached the supernatural, the unseen. This language makes use of material gifts which belong to the normal life of the offerers, and the offering of sacrifice is seen either as a divine command prescribed by the supernatural powers, or at least as a holy custom long since used in intercourse with the ancestors or the gods.

Secondly, the context in which a sacrifice is offered, or was first offered, if its nature is thought to be dependent on its history, will determine the purpose of the sacrifice in question.

In the history of eucharistic theology, these two factors have been consistently ignored. Sacrifice, a world-wide phenomenon, is not exclusively an act of propitiation. If the word Eucharist is identified as a propitiatory sacrifice, or rejected as a sacrifice because it is propitiatory, then it must be proved that its context is exclusively propitiatory. If we are discussing sacrifice, we should know what sacrifice is, and it is distressing that so many works have been written on the Christian Eucharist by scholars who have betrayed no understanding of either the meaning of sacrifice as a phenomenon, or even of the possible meaning of Semitic of Hebrew sacrifice. This is sad, for much debate about the Mass, the Eucharist, the Lord's Supper, need never have become a debate if the protagonists had taken the trouble to find out what sacrifice was at the outset. The milieu of the Western World is singularly ill-equipped to understand sacrifice and often is unaware that Christ lived in a culture that did understand sacrifice because it practised it. Yet Christians justify their practice of holding Eucharist from New Testament evidence, the command of Christ. One often feels that the real justification for beliefs and practices of the Eucharist derives from much more recent traditions and prejudices.

In the last chapter, the connection between the Last Supper and the Passover, whether as an anticipatory meal or as the celebration itself, has been indicated. It is also evident that the narratives of the Last Supper in the synoptic gospels and in I Corinthians have as their aim the proclamation of Christ as Passover lamb, deliverer and cleanser from sin. The synoptics see Christ as demonstrating by means of the Passover meal over which he presided, what he knew he would accomplish by his death. Both the synoptics and St Paul see the Last Supper as a proclamation of what Christ had done to and by generations of Christians after his death and resurrection. The accounts are not liturgical handouts or theological statements. They are proclamations of Christ's death (I Cor. 11.26). Through them is revealed that the Last Supper was both intimately related to the Crucifixion and also to Passover. Now we have already seen that Christ's death at Passover was seen by the gospel writers as the perfect Passover sacrifice for all people at all times, in which man communicated effectively with God through the matter of the man who was the perfect sacrifice. The Last Supper says this. Christ, according to the synoptics and St Paul, was saying at the Last Supper, 'I am Passover'. It has been suggested that the words 'Christ our Passover' of I Cor. 5.6–8 and the words 'Christ the first fruits' of I Cor. 15.20 were suggested to St Paul by the identification of Christ with Passover that took place at the Last Supper (Higgins 1952). The connection of Passover with covenant has also been explored in the previous chapter. Hence at the Last Supper Jesus is not only identifying himself with Passover but also with the covenant. The covenantal language does not need to be doubted, except for very good textual reasons, within the context of Passover. Within that context, the blood of the Passover lamb not only cleanses away sin but re-establishes the covenant. The Passover 'subsumed all time under the dominant event of the covenant' (Cooke 1969: 34). 'The interpretation of the Supper and the Passion in terms of the Covenant Sacrifice is deeply rooted in the New Testament' (Couratin 1955: 286).

The Last Supper was not only a proclamation: it was also an identification. This is of the very experience of sacrifice. Through the action of sacrifice there comes identification. God and man are identified in Christ in his sacrifice and Christ and his disciples are identified in the action of the Last Supper. This is why crude ideas of 'eat me' and 'drink me' are totally out of place in the Hebrew context of the Last Supper, as they are in Hebrew sacrifice. Jesus' words provoke no reaction of horror of cannibalism either from the disciples or from the early church simply because cannibalism or theophagy has no place in Hebrew sacrificial practice. Whatever the far-off ante-cedent motives might have been, no Hebrew thought he was either feeding, or feeding off, Yahweh in sacrifice. Hence Jesus could and did say 'This is my body' and 'This is my blood', with no fear of misunderstanding, because the words meant identification with him and with what he was about to accomplish. 'By eating and drinking he gives them a share in the atoning power of his death' (Jeremias 1966: 233). Again, as we have seen, there is no need to see Jesus as carefully weaving in the themes from the covenant sacrifice, the Day of Atonement sacrifice and the Passover sacrifice, since all these found their expression in Passover, and Passover, Atonement and Last Supper are bound together by Christ, certainly in the gospels and in St Paul.

Yet the Last Supper is not by itself the Atonement. What Christ did the night before he died and what he did by his death and by his whole life are related but not identical. What then is the relationship between Last Supper and Christ's own act of sacrifice? If he is the Passover lamb, what is there left for the Last Supper? The relation-ship between the Last Supper and the Cross is expressed in the same word as the relationship between the Passover and God's act of rescuing Israel from Egypt. In the New Testament this is the word *anamnesis*, translated in English by the word 'remembrance'. This is doubly unfortunate, since the main semantic areas of both the Greek and the English words are those of cerebral activity – either reminiscing, or the mental activity of bringing something to mind. In modern English there is the added area of sentiment attached to words connected with memory and remembering – nostalgia, '*à la recherche du temps perdu*', 'down memory lane' and so on. The Hebrew root *zkr* on the other hand is not concerned with cerebrating or with sentimentalizing. Its semantic area is that of relating, not just bringing to mind. Hence the nouns formed from the verb, *azkarah* and *zikkaron*, are concerned with renewing relationships, not just remem-bering them. So also, when the God of the Hebrews 'remembers' his people, he does not merely recall their existence to himself, or reminisce sadly about them. He does something about them, he renews his relationship with them, by either coming to their aid or by sorting them out. Just as the verb is most often used of God's initiative in 'remembering' Israel, so also the noun points to God's initiative. A remembrance is not 'a presentation before God intended to induce God to act' (Jeremias 1966: 249). Neither the Passover nor the Last Supper were reminders, *aides-mémoire* addressed to God, nor were they inducements to him to act. They renewed the relationship with God and identification with him established by God's initial act both in Egypt and in Christ. When the Hebrews kept Passover they had no intention of repeating the unrepeatable and escaping from Egypt all over again. Nor were they having an anniversary dinner. Similarly, when the disciples shared in the Last Supper, they were not repeating Calvary – they were hardly likely to have thought to do that proleptically: nor were they sentimentally holding a farewell dinner for a departing friend in the way portrayed in *Jesus Christ, Superstar*. The *eph'hapax* of Christ's own sacrifice is in no way threatened by the Last Supper any more than the *eph'hapax* of the mighty act of God in rescuing Israel from Egypt was threatened by Passover. Instead, the *anamnesis* of the Last Supper proclaims Christ's sacrifice and identifies those who hold supper with it. This it does, as had previously been done in the Passover, by means of sacrifice. To put it in other terms, man in Christ approaches God through the area of 'holy danger', and communication and understanding beginning with repentance and forgiveness is affected through sacrifice. Thus one sacrifice of one man is appropriated by all men in the sacrifice of the Last Supper. Hence the words, 'This is my body', 'This is my blood', identify Last Supper with Atonement, Christian community with Christ, their sacrifice with his. They sweep the disciples into the divine action of sacrifice. Those words are words of identification with action. They are not labels on exhibits in a museum. This is the disastrous mistake of scholastic and reformed theologians, to dispute static analyses of the eucharistic presence. Sacrifice is not a chemical experiment, converting one substance into another either totally or according to the accidents. Transubstantiation, consubstantiation, real presence, real absence, are all wide of the mark both of a sacrifice and of Semitic sacrifice. When an animal is sacrificed in Transkei, today, at no point does anyone present consider whether the tribal ancestors are present in the sacrificed beast or whether any act of transubstantiation has occurred. When a *zebach* was offered in Israel, at no point did anyone consider what had happened to the substance or accidents of the beast or its blood. Sacrifice is an action, not a chemical experiment. Behind the words 'This is my body/blood' lies the Hebrew copula, which would translate literally as 'This my body', 'This my blood' and is the word of identification of an offerer with his sacrifice. When the Nuer man lays his hand on his ox, he is not implying that he has changed into an ox or that he is physically part of the ox, but that he is identified with this ox, his sacrifice. So the words of Christ over bread and wine are words of identification, that his sacrifice is identified with their sacrifice, not that he is making an ontological statement about bread and wine. Sacrifice is not Holy Specie, but matter on its way to and from God. Jesus 'did not look upon His sacrifice as a thing apart from men, to be accepted passively as one recognizes an external event. On the contrary, He thought of it as standing in the closest relation to human need, as an experience to be shared and appropriated: and, as a realist, He provided a rite whereby fellowship in His sufferings and participation in the hallowing power of His sacrifice might be assured' (Taylor 1933: 125). The covenant is now applied to the people whom God has created in Jesus (Powers 1968). It may well be significant that Narsai in his *Liturgical Homilies* (in Widengren 1969) quotes the words of administration of communion as being 'the life of the King Christ'. Since Narsai came from Edessa, the capital of Syriac-speaking West Syria, it may well be that the dynamic identification of the Last Supper with Christ's act of sacrifice, and its life-giving effects had survived linguistically in this supremely Semitic area of the early Christian church. Similarly, the bread and the wine are called 'the life of God' in the Jacobite liturgy of Syria, and Ignatius of Antioch terms the Eucharist the 'medicine of immortality'.

Kilpatrick (1938) goes so far as to claim that there is no other way to describe the Eucharist than as sacrifice. Drawing on Jeremias's seminal work (1966: 237–55), *anamnesis* means, 'Do this in order that God may remember me and act'; it means proclamation, not repetition. He sees Luke's shorter text as original, the longer text being an attempt to eliminate references to blood (an early and common apologetic trend) and a reinforcing of the link with the Passover, an identification made by all three synoptics – John having the Passover as taking place *after* the Crucifixion and the Last Supper being, in John, a religious meal of Jesus' own solidarity, analogous to Qumran religious meals. Kilpatrick would agree with John, since no family was present at the Last Supper. He also points out that Paul could only have described the Eucharist as dangerous or lethal (bringing damnation), if taken wrongly, if he saw it as a sacrifice. No other meal could have that property. 'The one advantage a sacrifice has is that it can adjust itself to time and space' (1983: 110).

However, excursions into Semitic Christianity in patristic times make the assumption that the Lord's Supper was the Eucharist. This has been seriously challenged, and attention ought to be given to this challenge.

A case has been made for a non-connection between the Last Supper and the Eucharist as known in the sub-apostolic age. It has been pointed out that the liturgy known to the early church outside the New Testament consisted of prayer and thanks around a meal and was called the giving of gifts. 'This liturgy did not connect the Supper with the memorial of the death and the remembrance of Jesus' Last Supper' (Lietzmann 1953: 160). The case being put forward is that, even if the Last Supper were a Passover meal, or connected with one, the weekly celebration of the communion meal by the early Christians did not derive from the Last Supper but from some other source and only attracted to itself the character of and connection with the Last Supper at a much later date. Now it has to be admitted at the outset that very few references are made to sacrifice at all in the church fathers when they are discussing the Eucharist. Justin talks of a thanksgiving sacrifice and then proceeds to link it with the acceptable sacrifice offered by the Gentiles mentioned in Mal. 1.11. This is, of course apologetic and, as such is often to be found in patristic writings, the arguments being that the Jews did not produce sacrifices acceptable to God, whereas the Christians have fulfilled Malachi and through their Eucharist 'fragrant sacrifice and pure gifts are offered'. The Malachi passage was certainly concerned with the literal offering of sacrifices, but whether this constitutes proof that the Christian fathers saw the Eucharist as such is doubtful. The *Didache* speaks of the offerings of first fruits and Irenaeus sees the Eucharist as the new offering of the new covenant (*Adv. Haer* 4.17. 4–6). Throughout the pre-Cyprianic period there seems to be a tendency both to spiritualize sacrificial language even in connection with the Eucharist, and yet to use sacrifical terms, such as referring to the bishop as high priest (Hippolytus, *Didascalia*). There would perhaps be two conflicting tendencies at work. First there is the tendency to spiritualize sacrifice which is to be found in Greek intellectuals, and, by emulation, in

Hebrew and Christian writings. Hence it is unlikely that writers who considered their intellectual public (in effect, their reading public) would be keen to bring in sacrificial terminology, but would be more likely to exclude it. They would fear that their Eucharist could be misunderstood as some crude attempt at theophagy. Secondly, in their anti-Jewish apologetic they could not neglect sacrifice altogether, but would demonstrate that, backward though the Temple sacrifices might have been, they had been spiritually fulfilled, even superseded by Christ and in the liturgical practice of the Christians. The result is a dearth of sacrificial references. But it must also be made quite clear that there is in any case very little reference to the Eucharist in patristic writings as a whole. Eucharistic theology is very thin indeed. We have become used to a large section of any theological work being concerned with the Eucharist and this has been so since early medieval times in the West. We have also become used to the Eucharist being a major divisive factor between Christians. It is amazing and perhaps salutary to find that for almost four centuries, references to the Christian Eucharist are limited to four very brief accounts in the New Testament, a sprinkling of hazy and incidental comments on Christian offerings and a few sections in manuals of pastoralia. Much more is written about baptism in serious theology in the patristic age, and much, much more space is devoted to the nature and work of Christ and to Scripture. The fact is that nobody thought much about the Eucharist – they just did it. The Eucharist finds its place in liturgy, where liturgy is recorded, and in manuals of discipline. A characteristic of liturgy is that it tends not to be written down unless it is threatened with extinction and that comments upon it assume that the liturgy itself is well known: a characteristic of manuals of discipline is that they tend to concentrate on rules that have been breached in the past and not on what is accepted by all. All this contributed to a low incidence of reference to the Eucharist in early church records and a very low incidence of reference to sacrifice in connection with it. It may therefore seem an argument from silence, but the very liturgies themselves show that *oral* tradition and actual eucharistic practice gave the patristic age all it needed to know about the Eucharist. Also, it is only in the liturgies themselves that the tradition linking the Passover sacrifice and the Last Supper survived. This makes proof positive rather difficult. Added to all this was the fact that even the Jewish original had changed, since, after AD 70, the Passover lamb ceased to be part of the

Jewish Passover meal. Jesus in any case was the Lamb for Christians, and what remained of the Passover sacrifice looked to both Jew and Christian more like a meal for faithful people, a commemorative repast. Something that should have been obvious in Christian practice had been shamed into quiescence by the pressures of Greek philosophy – this something was sacrifice.

To the modern Westerner the Eucharist looks like a commemorative meal. Hence many have said that this is precisely what the Eucharist always was, that it had no connection with Passover or even with the Last Supper. Now before we get bowled over by this assumption it is well to set this argument within the broad stream of Christian tradition. As soon as clear description and liturgical summaries of the Eucharist begin to emerge, it is assumed that the Eucharist is the Last Supper, that Christians performing it are in fact obeying Christ's command to 'do this in remembrance of me'. No writer before the nineteenth century seriously denies this assumption. It is always possible that such a tradition is wrong, that oral tradition has gone astray. After all, there are many spurious explanations of well-known ceremonies. Yet in a matter like this, the onus is squarely on the critic to provide a better explanation, instead of depending on arguments from silence. It is, for example, a common argument to attribute the Eucharist, along with various other beliefs and practices, to St Paul, the great innovator, who also transformed a brilliant Rabbi into a world saviour. However feasible it is to see St Paul in this role, when he claimed to be the opposite, it is least feasible to see him 'inventing' the Eucharist. He says so little about the Last Supper and even less about Passover. Yet 'the Pauline form of the Eucharist proved to be from a later stage of the tradition, influenced by a type of Hellenistic sacramentalism akin to the ideas of the mystery religions' (so Kuhn 1958: 92). 'Hellenistic sacramentalism' sounds very imposing, but when actually identified it often means that the Eucharist was derived via St Paul from some Dionysiac, theophagic rite. Now Paul was a Jew. Even if he were familiar with Greek mystery cults, he does not give the impression that he was particularly impressed with Greek religion or anxious to take over its doctrine or cults. In fact, the evidence of influence of any sort of Hellenism upon New Testament Christianity is of the flimsiest. Judaism in its Palestinian form, the form known to Jesus himself, tended to reject anything Hellenistic. It would seem to be a much more likely estimate of the situation that, by the time Hellenistic ideas began to influence Christian thinkers, basic

Christian practices like the Eucharist were already established. In fact we can surely go as far as to assert that 'the Jewish origin of the Christian movement rendered it immune at the outset to the influences of the Mystery-cults' (Hooke 1956: 101). It is still possible that, since the Eucharist looked like a mystery cult to the outsider, as Pliny's evidence shows, it acquired something of the glamour of a *disciplina arcana*. Indeed Paul may well have used the word *musterion* to this end, though he does not use the word specifically of the Eucharist. The early Christians may well have exploited this symbolism as having the attractiveness of a mystery cult, though they seem to have done this much more in the context of baptism (Lupi 1975). We can safely assume that the Christian Eucharist was not an adaptation of a Hellenistic mystery cult.

Another theory which became popular after the discovery of the Dead Sea Scrolls is that, if we may not look for a Greek original for the Eucharist, we may look for a Jewish one instead, other than the Last Supper and the Passover. The Christian Eucharist is said to be an adaptation of the sort of sacramental meal practised at Qumran by the Jewish community there. Now this is perhaps another example of the search for any explanation but the obvious. No early Christian sources show any knowledge of Qumran, the New Testament makes not the slightest allusion to Qumran, and the Qumran documents make no mention of Jesus of Nazareth or of the Christians. Nor does internal evidence connecting Jesus with Qumran or Qumran with Jesus go beyond the unproven and the theoretical, though it is obviously proper to be prepared for such evidence to be discovered. Kuhn (1958) has advanced the hypothesis that the Eucharist emerged as a bread and wine meal from the sort of exclusive, silent bread meal, accompanied by prayer, practised by the community at Qumran. Apart from the massive lack of co-ordination in a comparatively small group of people in maintaining a tradition about a Last Passover supper while actually practising a friendship meal copied from a quite different Jewish milieu, there is no element of *anamnesis* in the Qumran meals (though there is an emphasis on covenant), the order is quite different, women were present, at least in attendance, wine was drunk and indeed played just as important a part as the bread (Jeremias 1966). In fact the connections are tenuous in the extreme, though it is perhaps over-censorious to say that 'such nonsense is an insult to the intelligence of his readers' (Rowley 1963: 266).

In all these theories it would seem that principles other than the desire for historical accuracy are at play: in other words, the sub-text is either the desire to avoid some particular brand of eucharistic theology or to impose some other pattern upon the Eucharist. For example, 'If an evolution really took place in Israelite sacrifice from an early fellowship meal to the idea of atonement by death only in later times, it is not a far step to the assumption that the Pauline interpretation of the Lord's Supper as a memorial of the death of Christ was a later development of what first had been a purely joyous fellowship meal' (quoted in Thompson 1963: 1). Indeed it is a far step, if not a goose step, to put together such a bewildering collection of missing links and *non sequiturs*. The facts are that a Last Supper is described in the New Testament as having all the characteristics of a Passover or pre-Passover meal. This meal then reappears in Christian practice all over Christendom as the Last Supper itself, now practised weekly, on the Day of the Lord's Resurrection, that day of his Passover victory. True, there is an intervening period between the New Testament and the earliest recorded liturgies of the Eucharist, in which references to this meal are sparse and confused – but then so are references to most things Christians did during this period. How likely is it that a changeling was substituted either by that wicked fairy, St Paul, or during the eucharistic 'tunnel period'? Christians ever since have believed that they had always obeyed Christ's command to 'do this in remembrance of me'. Is it likely that they were in fact doing something in remembrance of a Greek mystery cult or an Essene meal?

But there are also some pieces of evidence in favour of Christian tradition identifying the Eucharist with the Lord's Supper. First, the Quartodecimans took their stand on the observance of Easter on the date of Jewish Passover. They broke their pre-Passover fast with the Lord's Supper. They exhibit all the signs of a conservative group, unwilling to let go a precious calendar connection for the sake of a more convenient observance. But this was no quirk, nor was it pure conservatism like that of the Old Believers in Imperial Russia of a later period. For Melito of Sardis, the Passover connection was crucial, because there needs must be an assertion that Jesus was the Passover lamb, the deliverer, and the sacrifice he had commanded, the *anamnesis* he had prescribed, had taken the place of Jewish Passover, had fulfilled it. These celebrations *must* take place on that date however inconvenient. The Quartodecimans are in fact an unselfconscious witness to the Passover connection.

Secondly the very word 'Eucharist' is evidence in itself. The verb means 'to give thanks' and to apply it to the ensuing meal is about as natural as calling an English meal 'Grace'. The word or its synonym, *eulogein*, is used in the accounts of the Last Supper in the New Testament: its Hebrew equivalent is used of the prayers at the Passover meal, where it has been translate 'bless', though the Hebrew verb *barakh* is best translated 'to give thanks', when a human being is the subject and the deity the object; it is used in the narrative of the feeding of the five thousand and it virtually becomes a technical term for the Christian meal celebration in the sub-apostolic period, the oldest technical name for it as such. The problem with the word lies in its translation into English or Latin, where it has meant either too little or too much. Of course the Greek word means 'thanksgiving', but to leave the word in English merely as 'thanksgiving' is to choose the least dynamic equivalent possible and to violate all the rules of modern translation technique. For a start in its context it never meant just to say 'thank you'. Its Passover context makes it clear that it is a thanking-in-sacrifice – the Passover sacrifice. The Latin translation of *eucharistein* by *'gratias agere'* is no improvement and *'bona gratia'* in Aquinas is even worse, because it transforms a sacrifice into a statutory sacrament, coinage in a Grace bank. In fact, the very word 'sacrament' has a disastrous history in Western theology, is no substitute for sacrifice, and never was a viable translation of any Greek or Hebrew word on the subject.

Thirdly, there is the unanimous tradition of the liturgies themselves. Not only do they all assume that the Last Supper is the Christian Eucharist, that they are doing what Christ had ordered on the night before he died. They also assume that same dynamic relationship between what they do and what Christ did as is assumed by the Last Supper itself and by Passover in relation to Exodus/Sinai. In the liturgical life of the church itself, it is seen particularly in the description of the *Peregrinatio Etheriae*, that almost naive diary of a Spanish lady visiting Jerusalem. Easter is Resurrection Day: it is Christ's Passover: it culminates in the Easter Eucharist, introduced by the recital of the Exodus, which afterwards reached the Western church as the *Exultet*. The importance of the calendar as witness to the beliefs of those operating it should never be overlooked. The Passover sacrifice, Christ, the Lamb of God, made relevant through the sacrifice of the Eucharist, was demonstrated to Christians of the early centuries by what they saw acted out in front of them in the pageantry of the developing Christian year. This is a factor which will be much more easily perceived by Orthodox Christians than by Westerns, for 'In the Greek church, the eucharistic sacrifice was far richer in meaning than is implied by the transactional character of the Western Mass' (Taylor 1968: 408). It should be added that it is not the character of the Western liturgy itself that is transactional, but the theology that has all too often accompanied it. Dix (1945: 281) accuses both John Chrysostom and Theodore of Mopsuestia and by implication, the Eastern liturgies of having a passive Christ who is then activated by the Spirit. In making this charge, Dix has ignored much very useful evidence concerning the real beliefs and practices of the Antiochene church. One suspects that his views are coloured by his easy assumption that he is dealing with an arch-heretic in Theodore and a muddled thinker in Chrysostom, and that he is concerned to defend the words of institution as the moment of consecration against all comers, the *epiklesis* included. Chrysostom speaks of the Spirit coming upon the elements and 'you see the Lamb sacrificed and consummated' (*Hom. in Coemet. et Cruc.* 3, 401D). This is seen by Dix as a contradiction of Chrysostom's other thought about Christ as the heavenly high priest. In fact it goes with it perfectly, since both come from the Epistle to the Hebrews with its imagery of Christ in heaven both as the perfect priest and as the triumphant Lamb, sacrificed and perfected. This is not passive, but triumphant and passes on into the Eastern Orthodox tradition as the Eucharist in which the triumphant Christ, already sacrificed, communicated his glory to his church. Another nugget of Chrysostom loses out completely by dint of faulty translation. 'This word once spoken at every altar in the churches from that day until this and until He come, *maketh perfect* (*apartismenen ergazetai*) the sacrifice' (*Prod. Judae* 1.6, 384 BC). Now the usual verb used about perfecting as applied to Christ is *teleioō*. This one means more to 'make a perfect fit', hence 'to render relevant'. The 'word' that Chrysostom is talking about makes the sacrifice relevant to the present church. Now this is precisely the work of the Holy Spirit from Pentecost onwards, to take Christ and relate him to church and world. Far from having a passive view of Christ at the Eucharist, Chrysostom sees Word or Spirit moving from Christ's perfected sacrifice and rendering it operative, relevant in the Eucharist to the later Christian church. It is significant that Chrysostom belongs to the Antiochene tradition, that tradition most influenced by Semitic thought and least afraid of the language of sacrifice. With this in mind we can unravel what Theodore of Mopsuestia had to say about the Eucharist of his day. In his commentary on the action of the Eucharist, Theodore describes how the ceremonies of the *prothesis* (before the Eucharist proper begins) represent the slaughtering of Christ, how, adored by angels under the guise of deacons, the corpse of Christ is laid on the altar with all reverence at the offertory, and how, to Dix's horror, this is called by Theodore 'offering (*anaphora*)' and 'sacrifice', much too early on, while Christ is representationally dead, and before the consecration. Dix explains this as a muddled confusion by Theodore of his own ideas and a rite that is not to be explained in this way, and bewails the fact that some of Theodore's ideas appear to have found their way into the Byzantine liturgies and into the Orthodox church. He warns his readers against this, on the grounds that there are enough muddles in the Anglican prayer-book Eucharist already without importing Orthodox ones to add to the confusion.

Part of Dix's misunderstanding is due to his search for a moment of consecration, a pardonable enough misunderstanding, when so many Orthodox theologians have tried to emulate their Western brothers in looking for such a moment and in producing their own counterblast – the *epiclesis*. But there is a deeper misunderstanding. This lies in that what Theodore is really doing is showing that the whole life of Christ, his sacrifice consummated at Calvary and Easter, is portrayed, made real, in the Eucharist. This is *anamnesis* spelled out in practical terms, a masterly parallel to the Passover liturgy of the Jews, in which all the events of the escape from Egypt are together brought to bear on later generations of Israelites through the Passover sacrifice. This is effected by the Holy Spirit. Theodore has no intention of suggesting that Christ becomes a corpse again at each Eucharist. Christ's whole life, his sacrifice, is applied to the church over which Theodore presides, through the Eucharist. The material of sacrifice, the bread and the wine are the means through which the holiness of Christ's sacrifice of a life is communicated to the people and through these materials they are identified with all the acts of Christ's life. The Holy Spirit is not seen as performing a 'transaccidentation' (Dix's incredible word for putting over the unsuspecting Theodore's thought). He is the agent of Christ's incarnation, making the whole Christ and his sacrifice relevant to the church. Christ, far from being a passive victim (the very word 'victim' is out of place) is the triumphant priest and sacrifice whose life is actively made relevant through the Spirit in the offering of sacrifice by the people of God. The term 'offering of sacrifice', is to be found in Hippolytus, Cyril of Jerusalem and the liturgy of Addai and Mari, all with likely Antiochene connections. Far from being the muddled allegorizing of a heretical soul, Theodore's sermons shed added light on the Christian Eucharist, for he is commenting on what he had received, that the Eucharist is the Christian Passover, celebrating, in the language of sacrifice, what Christ did in the offering and receiving back of that wonderful life.

Fifthly, it has often been said that a jump from a yearly Passover to a weekly Eucharist is inexplicable, except in terms of some origin of the Eucharist apart from the Last Supper. In fact this is to be explained by the way in which the Christians exulted in having a true and better Passover than the Jews and also in making their Passover their very own. This came in their use of the calendar. The Jewish year was a highly developed one, proclaiming their mystery of redemption. The Christian church seems both to have taken this year over and made it their own and to have added a weekly cycle of celebration, amply witnessed to in Justin, in which they took the day of the Lord's resurrection and kept their Passover upon it. So strong was this tradition that it must have been the most potent reason for inducing the Roman church and even finally the Quartodecimans to accept a permanent Sunday as the day of the week for Easter.

Finally, Cooke (1960) gives five characteristics of the Last Supper. It was a fraternal meal, at which Judas's treason was especially heinous. It was a paschal meal bound also to the Sinai covenant. It was a messianic action, linking Christ's personal action and death, his new covenant, with the Last Supper. It was a founding of the kingdom of God and belonged to that eschatological present and future. It was a hierarchical affair, at which Jesus presided as head of a new Passover family. All these characteristics are prominent in early liturgies. Not all of these characteristics are to be found in either mystery cults or Qumran meals. It is surely right that we trust the tradition of the church in its simplest assertion, that they were doing what they had been told to do by Christ at his Passover, in *anamnesis* of him and of all that he had accomplished.

When people carry out practices almost instinctively, there is always the danger that someone at some time in the future will ask the reason why things are being done, and even more danger that the explanation then given will be either partial or faulty. By the fourth century AD the Christian church included very few people of Jewish descent: it did include a sizeable group of people of Semitic descent – Syrians and the like, but in the Byzantine Empire, Greek thought and practice dominated, while in the West, Semitic influence survived only in biblical tradition, and, perhaps, in a rather distorted form in Donatism in North Africa. This meant that the church inherited a cultus that was sacrificial and a theology that ignored sacrifice, or very occasionally used sacrificial terms about Christ's own actions, terms inherited from the New Testament writers, and in turn from the Old Testament. This is the hiatus that bedevils the subject of sacrifice in the Christian church. The biblical writers assume that their readers know all about it and do not explain it, while later Christian writers either assume it or set off on explanations of their own that do not tally with Hebrew ideas and practice. The Greco-Roman world had little or no help in understanding sacrifice coming from other quarters either. The Greek and Roman public sacrifices had long since become discredited in the eyes of intelligent people, while Hebrew sacrifices belonged to the past, with the Jerusalem Temple destroyed, never to be rebuilt, and even Passover, minus its lamb, looked more like a banquet than a sacrifice.

There are various examples which can be quoted from some of the Post-Nicene Greek fathers which show tendencies to identify the Eucharist with Christ's sacrifice. For example, 'When you sacrifice the Master's body and blood with bloodless knife' (Gregory of Nazianzus, *Ep.* 171), Cyril of Jerusalem's reference to the Eucharist as a sacrifice for the propitiation of sin (*Mystagogical Catecheses* 5.8–10), Chrysostom's references to the Eucharist as the sacrifice of Christ (*Hom. in Heb.* 17.3, 169A), although his actual words are 'we make the memorial of the sacrifice'. These examples have been quoted as tendencies in the Greek fathers towards identifying the Eucharist as some sort of re-enactment or representation of Christ's sacrifice. Yet it would seem, from Chrysostom's actual words, from the sermons of Theodore of Mopsuestia already referred to, and from the tradition of the Eastern church ever since, that in Eastern Christianity they were capable of seeing the difference between a drama and a historical repetition, an act of sacrifice and its *anamnesis*. That they did in fact not think of Christ as being re-sacrificed, or re-presented, or his work of offering added to in any way may be due to a variety of factors, including the liturgy itself. It may also be that Theodore's type of comment upon the liturgy was very widely accepted and prevented a literal identification of the Eucharist with some sort of actual repetition of all aspects of Christ's sacrifice.

Be this as it may, it is in the West that we find a recovery of the sacrifice of the Eucharist – in a strange and alarming way. It is common to trace this tendency back to a remark of St Cyprian of Carthage, 'The Lord's Passion is the sacrifice we offer' (*Ep.* 63.9). Cyprian was talking primarily about the priesthood (yet another example of the Eucharist entering patristic theology as a side-assumption rather than as a main topic) and is contrasting the Jewish priesthood with that of Christ and of the Christian ministry. Cyprian is also said to be 'no theologian', a useful let-out, and it is in any case open to doubt just how much influence his remark in fact had upon the development of eucharistic doctrine. Nevertheless he said it, or wrote it and it marks a very great divide. Gone is the association of Eucharist with Passover: gone also is the identification of the Eucharist with all the acts of Christ's life. We are on our way to identifying sacrifice with that aspect of sacrifice, which is least repeatable in Christ's sacrifice – expiation, or even propitiation.

This is not the place to give a history of the development of the doctrine of the sacrifice of the Eucharist in the Catholic West. This has been better undertaken elsewhere (Masure 1954). There are, of course caveats. Popular beliefs, reflected in prayer manuals, are not to be taken as the faith of the church. Even in an institution as monochrome as Post-Tridentine, pre-Vatican II, Rome, there is still some room for variations of opinion. The liturgy itself tends to be more conservative than either popular opinion or theological state-ments. There is little support in the text of the Roman Mass, even before its recent revisions, for theological interpretations that later became identified with the Mass and were so vehemently attacked as constituting the Mass, itself. We will limit this part of the study to a few landmarks, with these caveats in mind and at the risk of presenting a highly unbalanced view of the Eucharist in the West.

'*In nova lege verum Christi sacrificium communicatur fidelibus sub specie panis et vini*' (St Thomas Aquinas, *Summa Theologica* 3, qu. 22 art. 6). This is the Latin version of the meaning of *anamnesis*, but the words '*communicatur*' and '*specie*' are highly inadequate for this purpose. One is sometimes almost driven to the conclusion that Latin is a language ill-adapted to the needs of theology.

But apart from the problem of language, there is the confusion over sacraments and sacrifice. It has somehow been accepted that a sacrament, which is in effect the state of affairs produced by a sacrifice, gives more security than a sacrifice and avoids confusion

with the finality of what Christ did on the Cross. The Eucharist 'is not
the repetition of the sacrifice, nor is it the completion of the sacrifice; it
is simply the sacrifice itself, present in the unique mode of a sacrament,
present, that is, simply and solely because the sacramental species are
the divinely ordained effective signs of it' (Mascall 1953: 96). In this
statement the Eucharist has been turned into a sort of precipitate of
Christ's sacrifice. The Eucharist is not in fact the sacrament of Christ's
sacrifice – it is what the Last Supper says it is, the *anamnesis* of his
sacrifice, the whole sacrifice of the life of Christ made relevant, through
the offering of bread and wine, by dominical command, to the present
Christians, who are then identified with him.

The word 'immolation' has, both before and after the Council of
Trent, done tremendous harm in the debate on the Eucharist. An
immolation is the slaughtering of a sacrifical victim. In Western
eucharistic theology this immolation has inevitably been linked with
propitiation. Hence Christ has been seen as immolated in order to
propitiate God's anger, and, when this one-sided atonement theology
reached the Eucharist, this also was seen as an immolation to propitiate
God. Now it's difficult enough for a Westerner to see what the Passover
sacrifice is in relation to the Exodus, without introducing immolation
into it. How can an immolation *not* be repeated? The fact is that there is
an underlying confusion between the priorities in sacrifice and
priorities in one unique sacrifice, that of Christ himself. In sacrifice, the
death of the animal or the burning of the loaf is incidental to the action
itself: it is part of a wider and deeper action. In Christ's sacrifice his
death became a top priority in the action – he had to die. At the Last
Supper his death is proclaimed, proclaimed as having been achieved
once and for all – like the Lamb standing, slain, on the heavenly altar in
the Apocalypse. There is no immolation at the Eucharist but the
celebration, the proclamation of an immolation. This is what *anamnesis*
is all about – the relating of Christ's whole life and acts through the
sacrifice of the bread and the wine to the present participants, just as the
events of the Exodus were communicated through the Passover meal to
those Jews then present. Life is shared, but there does not have to be an
immolation. The Eucharist only has immolation in that it identifies and
rests upon the one true pure immortal immolation.

'There is a tradition of recent origin – it would seem to go no further
back than de Lugo – found in manuals of theology and pulpit
instructions, which persists in regarding the putting to death of the
victim or its combustion or libation, as essentially negative acts

performed for the purpose of destroying it – and at times even of annihilating it – to give honour and glory to the sovereign Master of life and death, of being and non-being' (Masure 1954: 156). This is perfectly true, except that it does go further back than de Lugo and does continue today, unabashed by the strictures of Masure. It has escaped out of some pocket book of definitions and roams about in eucharistic belief hand in hand with immolation.

In reaction quite rightly against these ideas, which to him suggested that the offering of the Eucharist by the priests of the church not only repeated the offering of Christ himself, but virtually unsurped the place of his sacrifice, Calvin would only accept a sacrifice of thanksgiving for the Eucharist. Unfortunately the meaning he gave to the phrase, 'sacrifice of thanksgiving' was not that of the Old Testament, but the etiolated meaning of the term which occurs in a few New Testament contexts, not those of the Last Supper, and again in some sub-apostolic documents, which do refer to the Last Supper. However Calvin clearly saw the Eucharist in covenantal terms, and if he had but pursued this line of thought it could well have led him from the Last Supper to the Passover. Instead, however, he totally obscured the issue by insisting on the unbiblical distinction between a sacrifice and an offering. The Reformation debate about the Eucharist was so concerned to root out medieval distortions that it accepted scholastic definitions and terms instead of examining them. This was doubtless one of the limitations of the period. In the sixteenth century, Europeans had little or no data to go on concerning sacrifice. They knew that Christ had offered himself and that his blood took away sins – in a propitiatory way: this was the legacy of late medieval theology. They also knew that the Mass was said to be a repeated sacrifice, in which the priest had the power to do away with sins (which otherwise would send anyone straight to Hell) by re-offering Christ upon the church's altars. Against this some reacted, seeing in it the tyranny of the priesthood and a deadly arrogance in presuming that anyone had any right whatever to offer Christ afresh, especially in chantry chapels, 'for the wealthy dead'. They had no knowledge of what Hebrew sacrifice had meant or done: they did not realize that the mercenary approach to sacrifice they detested had been long ago condemned in old Israel. They knew of no contemporary people who still offered sacrifice, since Islam outside Mecca did not so, and they would have written it off as pagan and useless if they had known of any examples. It is no wonder therefore that they rejected the sacrifice of the Mass as blasphemous. The scandal is that there are so many thinking Christians today, with so many resources open to them in anthropology and Semitic studies, who still remain on the sixteenth century battlefield.

An issue that has long since bedevilled the whole debate concerning the Eucharist in the West has been the mode of Christ's presence in the bread and wine. The origins of this debate are traceable academically to the various adaptions of Greek philosophical theories concerning matter. The most well-known of these is the famous theory of transubstantiation. But under the academic theories lies a far more serious change in the attitude of Christians towards acts of God. It is part of a general unwillingness to trust God, so that cast-iron certainties, gilt-edged stock must be sought for in visible objects, such as the inerrant book or the guaranteed sacraments. The idea of sacraments as unfailing repositories of Godhead is totally foreign to Hebrew theology and to the practice of sacrifice itself. In sacrifice man meets up with the superhuman: he communicates with the superhuman by means of sacrifice. It is the act of sacrifice, not the substance employed that breaks through the holy danger threshold. True, blood is holy, as are, to a lesser extent, other parts of the sacrificed object. But they are only holy because they are in process of being sacrificed, not *per se*. Christ is never presented to us as a static being in the New Testament, either as a Nestorian 'Strephon', part God and part man, or as a Eutychian divine owner/occupier of a human body, but as God and man in action together in a perfect life of obedience to God, offered as sacrifice to make and to demonstrate the unity between God and man. The Eucharist must share that dynamic nature of sacrifice. It is the *anamnesis* of Christ's sacrifice. It is the *rite de passage* provided for the Christian church in order that it may share in that supreme *rite de passage* in which man in Christ, impelled by the Spirit, passes as a sacrifice through 'holy danger.'

In the original versions of the ancient Christian liturgies, including the Roman rite, there are no set confessions of sins or expressions of penitence. These, in both East and West, are later additions. There is much thanksgiving for sins forgiven, but penitence would appear to be taken for granted. Now this phenomenon must have an explanation. It obviously cannot mean that Christians up to the time of St Bernard either had no sins to be forgiven or imagined that they were sinless, or thought that their sins did not matter. There was plenty of penitence in Christians and there were debates about penitence too –

Augustine is ample testimony to that. But it did not find its way into the eucharistic liturgy until comparatively late. It may well be that there is a connection between the growing assumption that the Mass was an expiatory sacrifice and the addition of forms of confession and absolution to the liturgy – forms which, in the Roman rite, even introduced a separation between priestly and lay penitence. In the first centuries of the Christian church, the more natural link would be between Christ's expiation of sin and the act of *baptism*, not the Eucharist. Enough has been said already about the preliminary nature of expiation in the total drama of sacrifice. Baptism is likewise the preliminary act, or if this seems to depreciate baptism, the first step in the identification of the Christian with Christ. The obvious symbolism of washing with water meant, particularly to an adult convert, that Christ's sacrifice was now applied to him for the cleansing from sin. Afterwards he went on to the full celebration of the victorious sacrifice of Christ's life, triumphantly vindicated at Easter. In fact the Easter baptisms, followed by the Easter Eucharist, constituted the whole *anamnesis* in liturgy of Christ's sacrifice. Eucharist without baptism could not show this forth adequately, and the need for penitence to be actually expressed – a sort of apology for the full penitence of baptism – began to creep in to a rite shorn of its natural first act, that of water baptism. The phrase from the Apocalypse 'washed in the blood of the Lamb' sounds and always did sound quite revolting if taken literally – no Hebrew sacrifice involved washing in blood, and there is no evidence at all to make us suspect that some Greek mystery rite initiation ceremony is in the mind of the writer, 'Washed in the blood of the Lamb' starts from the shedding of Christ's blood and shows this as fulfilled in the water of baptism. The baptism–Eucharist of the early centuries of the Christian church, practised actively on new converts, but witnessed and shared by all church members, is the full *rite de passage*, which depends on the act of Christ in his whole life from birth, through baptism in Jordan to Cross and resurrection. Hence the Eucharist by itself was never seen as an *anamnesis* of expiation – this was the place of baptism. Together they marked the passage from death and life – as sacrifice does, for sacrifice is concerned with death and life. Christian sacrifice starts with death, but cannot but end in the proclamation of life. Christ's death is proclaimed as giving life. '"I am not worthy that thou shouldest come under my roof", "Then will I go unto the altar of God" are *one* celebration and one act of God' (Van der Leeuw: 359). 'Jesus looked upon His suffering and death as the fulfilment of a divine purpose, in which His will was at one with that of the Father, and in virtue of which He accepted an active vocation connected with the Rule of God. He thought of His death as a victorious struggle with the powers of evil, and interpreted His suffering, in relation to men, as representative and vicarious in a sacrificial ministry which involved participation in the consquences of human sin. So far, however, was He from thinking of His Messianic work as automatic and self-acting in its results that He provided a rite whereby men should be able to share in the power of His surrendered life and make his offering their own' (Taylor 1937: 270–1).

SEVEN

FILLING UP THE SACRIFICE

Sacrifice and suffering are not normally intimately connected. The sufferings of the slaughtered animal, or of the burnt vegetable, or even of the immolated human being, have not generally been taken into consideration by the sacrificing community. Nor has the suffering of the victim been a significant motive in the abandoning or commuting of sacrificial practices. This applies just as much to Hebrew sacrifices as those of other peoples. The *aqedah* did not stop short of the actual death of Isaac for compassionate reasons. Concern for the feelings of Abraham, Sarah or Isaac is evinced only in commentaries of a much later period. In the same way the offering of animals in the Temple at Jerusalem did not cease for humanitarian reasons, but simply because the Temple was in ruins and all sacrifice apart from that of the Passover Lamb had to be done in the Temple alone.

There is, however, one place in the Old Testament where sacrifice and suffering come together decisively – in the person and experience of the servant. The theories that have been advanced concerning the identity of the servant, about the relationship between the passages describing him and the surrounding text, about the date of writing of Isa. 40–55, are all many and varied. Philip in Acts 8 put forward the first definite theory about the servant's identity, and theories have been appearing ever since, particularly during the last 200 years.

Certain assumptions need to be made before we proceed to outline the juxtaposition of sacrifice and suffering in the servant. These are commonly held assumptions and are equally commonly contested. They do not necessarily affect the claims about to be made concerning the role of the servant, but they provide a framework, and arguments about them would belong rather to a full-scale commentary on the book of Isaiah. For present purposes, therefore, we assume:–

(*a*) that Isa. 40–55 belongs to the exilic period and that the references to Cyrus are contemporary with that period.

(*b*) that Isa. 40–55, whatever its relationship to the first 39 chapters of the book of Isaiah, or to the last 11 chapters, is all of one piece structurally and theologically. It is a call to faith in God, addressed to the community in exile. The 'servant-songs' are integral to the chapters as a whole and should not be detached from their surroundings.

(*c*) that the royal psalms were already in use in the Temple before 586 and that they and the tradition they represent must have been known to the unknown prophet.

(*d*) that we reject Whybray's analysis of Isa. 53 as a thanksgiving psalm for a liberated prophet (1978) in which even the actual death of the servant is denied as having taken place.

The major themes of these chapters are the utter reliability of the Lord God, the Creator: his continuing election of Israel as his people, to be restored shortly to their land by God's unwitting servant, Cyrus the first emperor of Persia: his demand that his people remain faithful to him alone in terms of the covenant and that therefore the worship of idols in all its stupidity is not to be tolerated; and the renewed calling of Israel, even though they see themselves as stripped of their identity by their resettlement in Babylon.

Into this renewed calling of Israel to be God's people under changed circumstances, comes the servant motif. At times he appears to be identified with Israel without qualification (e.g. Isa. 49.3) and at other times he appears to have a life of his own and a ministry apart from that to Israel. Most of all this would be the subject matter for any modern commentary on Isa. 40–55.

However it is put forward as a serious claim here that the secret of the servant's identity and his role lies in the role of the king in Judah before 586. This is a link usually dismissed by commentators and certainly played down, but it is in fact the only identification of the servant that does not do violence either to the plain meaning of some of the text or to the known traditions of Hebrew theology. (To enlarge on this point, the identification of the servant with a figure from the past or in the future in such language as is used has no parallel in fact or fiction. Likewise the identification of the servant with Israel, real or ideal, simply does not fit what is said about him in many of the passages.) The royal psalms demonstrate the sacral nature of the Hebrew monarchy, at least in the Southern kingdom. They show that the king had a special relationship to Yahweh, that he was 'the royal son' (Ps. 72.1). He has a Janus function in that he represents Israel before God, both within the Temple and outside it. He also ministers God's rule to Israel. He represents Israel to the world of nations, whether they take any notice of him or not. In his office and person he does for the world of nations whatever God wants Israel to be and to do. In particular he, the king, is to exercise 'the option for the poor' to curb those who oppress the poor, to bring God's justice to God's people and to demonstrate this in the power of the Lord to the nations. All this has been shown quite clearly in the works of Mowinckel (1962) and de Vaux (1961). The so-called royal theology 'trajectory' pursues its course through the Old Testament tradition, not as a socially oppressive ideology (though it could become so in the hands of rulers such as Jehoiakim), but as a 'liberation theology'. The king's function was to be that of continuing liberator, concerning himself with the poor and oppressed within Israel and with the enlightenment of the nations outside Israel.

This 'royal trajectory' or royal theology would have been ready to hand for the prophet of the exile to use. Our contention here is that this is what he did. He took the royal theology and applied it to Israel in the new circumstances, not as a hope for a restored monarchy, but as a challenge addressed to the whole community, which had already, over the centuries up to 586 seen itself as represented in the person and role of the monarch. The prophet's message is, 'God is still your ruler. Trust him because he is the Creator. Avoid all idolatry because it is both idiotic and an affront to the Lord. Your election is still valid, even though you reside far away from your promised land. Your task, God-given, is that of your king who used to represent you. You are to practise justice within Israel in the land to which you are to be restored. You are to be a light to the nations.' Thus two trajectories, or two covenantal traditions – God in covenant with the people in their twelve tribes, and God in covenant with the people enshrined in his covenant with the house of David (Isa. 55.3) – are brought together in one message or reassurance. The servant is therefore Israel as expressed in the monarchs of the house of David, whether to be restored to a throne in Jerusalem or not. The servant is quite naturally sometimes a corporate personality, sometimes an individual, just as in the royal psalms it is not always easy to determine whether the royal references are being made to the monarch, to the King of kings or to Israel-expressed-in-her-king.

What follows from this is a new and shocking role for king and people. Both king and people must now accept a new calling to be expressed in suffering and in sacrifice. Having undergone the totally humiliating experience of loss of identity in the debacle of 586, Israel must now move on to a new understanding of her calling, in which the triumph belongs not to Israel herself but solely to God. In this new vision, Israel is the servant, prepared to undergo humiliation and suffering and to be herself the sacrifice or at least the opening movement of the sacrificial symphony, through which the alienation of the world of nations from its true Lord and Creator (as opposed to the false idol-lords attacked so vigorously by the prophet) is to be removed. This is the kingship of the future, the leadership that will open the way through sacrifice for the world of nations to approach its Lord. The fact that Israel, after Isaiah's prophetic writings, showed very little sign of having heard the message does not affect the interpretation put upon it here. Many messages are unheard or ignored or misunderstood by the actual communities for which they are intended. Isaiah was saying, 'I show you a new way to fulfil your election by your Lord – the way of sacrifice, involving suffering and death.' This is the kingly path, not one of national triumph or self-sufficiency. Dare it be said that the way of holocaust is the way for Israel and her king according to the prophet? Far from provoking Jewish theologians to atheism, the holocaust of the Second World War, whether accepted or not, is a fulfilment of Isaiah's plan for Israel and should be a message to the Christian Church that, if they really consider themselves to be the new Israel, this is what they must accept for themselves – sacrifice, suffering and holocaust. After all the very word 'holocaust' means a burnt-offering, totally consumed by fire. This is the *telos* of the royal trajectory and this is true kingship. No wonder that Christians from the earliest times hailed Jesus as king and as Israel, precisely because he claimed to have done what the king-servant-people of Israel was supposed to have done.

The prophet reveals his plan in stages moving from where he thinks Israel is to where he thinks that God wants her to be. He starts from where Israel is, firmly within the tradition of the royal psalms and probably hoping for a speedy restoration of the dynasty of David. His theology is one of weaning Israel away from misguided hopes and expectations to a new understanding of her purpose. The language of Isa. 42 resembles in places that of Ps. 72. The traditional invocation of God's spirit upon the king is now applied to the servant and thereby to Israel. Israel in her kingly-servant role will bring forth justice to the nations. The similarities between Isa. 42. 1–4 and Ps. 72 have not been sufficiently recognized, though McKenzie (1967: iii) pointed out significantly that the servant 'is the figure who recapitulates in himself all the religious gifts and the religious mission of Israel . . . . He is the fullness of Israel. In him the history of Israel reaches its achievement.' To an Israelite of the time of the exile, on hearing or reading the message of these chapters, what single figure could be embodied in the description of the servant of Isaiah 42, *but* that of the king? It is extremely fanciful to see the contemporary Israelite in the prophet's time making an identification of the servant with some great figure of the past or even of the future without some very clear indication that the prophet was meaning him to imagine Moses, or Jeremiah or Cyrus. Similarly, a contemporary Israelite would have no difficulty in a corporate identity of the servant with Israel but would have needed a great deal of help to identify the servant with any group within Israel, such as the righteous remnant. There is in fact no other equation of a person (singular) with Israel (corporate) that makes sense in what we know of the sixth century BC apart from the king. The royal trajectory did not plummet in 586 any more than, say, the tradition of the Hapsburg plummeted in Central Europe in 1917. But Isaiah says that Israel, the community as a whole, must now accept the burden of kingship. She must now bring forth justice to the nations 'with a gentleness like that of God himself' (Smart 1965: 79). This theme is developed in chs. 49 and 50. Israel's attitude must be that of disciple, painstaking teacher, not conquering king, victorious general.

It comes as less of a surprise that the purpose of Israel's election and very existence is effected, not by a campaign of annihilation, by another Joshua invasion, but by the servant-king-Israel being offered as an *'asham* with all the disgrace, humiliation and hurt that accompanies death by immolation. The Holy War theme is now left far behind and with it should also be left, particularly for Christians, the curse of present-day politics, pride of nation or race. Christians are *not* called upon to claim that *their* nation is God's bounteous gift to grateful humanity – and this applies equally well to such claims as are made for British Raj, for '*La France, mère des arts, des armes et des lois*', for '*die wonder van Afrikaans*' and for 'Black is beautiful'. The role of servant-king-Israel-Christendom is not perfectly expressed in a Crusade or a Christian national anything but in sacrifice-in-suffering. It cannot be accidental that the word '*asham* is used of the servant's future role in Isa. 53.10. Here, in the servant, cultus and covenant receive their fullest expression. God's purpose is finally achieved in the offering of king and people of Israel in one final '*asham*. The sacrifice can now be completed. This is the offering which Israel was born for and destined to offer. 'Unless Israel accepts the servant as its incorporation it cannot keep faith with Yahweh' (McKenzie, 1967: iii).

In the servant, sacral kingship and covenant people of God are fused in one act of sacrifice. New vistas are opened up. Sacrifice and suffering are now linked together. Jesus did not make an obvious identification of himself with the servant: rather he made the identification of himself with the suffering of all people in his use on the Cross of the lament Psalm 22. It remained for the continuing presence of Jesus, the church, to make the identification of Jesus with the king who suffers in order to become the universal sacrifice – the '*asham* that precedes the Lamb of the Passover, offered by all the people who have accepted liberation by him.

The second and very important issue is the continuation of the sacrificial act in the life of the community that no longer has a demonstrable 'victim' to offer. What of the Christian Church? Most of it no longer offers animals or cereals. Is sacrifice, in effect, a thing of the past? The claim is being made here that, in the hands of the theologians of the New Testament, sacrifice, far from being treated as otiose, acquires a wider meaning and a staying power. This happens, *not* because Paul and the others regarded sacrifice as an unworthy concept in their modern age (as many of the church fathers may well have thought), but that they saw it as the way *par excellence* in which Christ's life, rendered up and given back, restored the cosmos to its glory. Even if Calvary becomes a distant event and even if the *anamnesis* of Calvary becomes a symbolic ritual act difficult to connect with its original, the whole meaning and continuing application of the sacrifice lives on in the way he intended it to live on – in his Body of Sacrifice.

It has been a serious fault in both patristic and contemporary, twentieth century, theology, that either sacrifice has been limited to one hour a week in a consecrated building and to a wafer and a drop of fortified wine, or else Calvary has been applied to the contemporary scene as a set of ethical precepts and advice for social action, flowing from the example of a heroically dead Messiah. In fact Christ clearly indicated just how his unique sacrifice should continue to be offered. His instruction: 'Do this in remembrance of me' is not remarkable for its liturgical directions, but for the fact that he is showing a community of his disciples just how, in the future, they are to offer sacrifice. This is his body, existing to be offered on and for the world as he had offered his body.

Let us examine the ways that sacrificial language is used, outside the gospels, and, obviously, excluding its occasional use in connection with pagan cults.

Paul wrote (Rom. 12. 1), 'I appeal to you therefore, brethren, by the mercies of God, to present your bodies as a living sacrifice, holy and acceptable to God, which is your spiritual service.' At first glance this might seem to be a 'spiritualizing' of sacrifice, as if Paul were avoiding a reference to actual cultic sacrifice and implying that Christians, unlike Jews or pagans had moved away into a more intangible, intellectual, ethical and moral meaning. This is certainly what many schools of atonement theology would like us to make of this passage. This new metaphorical sacrifice will now replace the old bloody sacrifices, since Christ's perfect self-offering is now complete and no vestige of the crudity of sacrifice remains.

This 'spiritualization' ignores the place of the text within the epistle as a whole. It lies between St Paul's proclamation of what Christ has accomplished and the invitation to the Christian community (at Rome and elsewhere) to respond to that sacrifice in faith and behaviour. He then turns to his own people, the Jews, and outlines his own hopes for them in Christ. He then explains to the Christian community how Christ's act has worked out for them and how they must respond to it as a community. Here, in Romans, Paul has finished his exposition of Christ's mighty and all-powerful sacrifice and our response to it. He has now turned to its outworking within the community, the body. Christ's sacrifice is made. How are they to live it out? Now, at this point Paul deliberately uses sacrificial language. He says, 'Present (*parastēsai*, a technical term for the presenting of sacrifices, though not used in this way in the Septuagint) your bodies as a living sacrifice.' This use of bodies is in contrast to the 'body of sin' referred to earlier in the epistle. The bodies (persons) of the believers are now fit for sacrifice, but they are to be a living sacrifice (*thusian zōsan*): they will remain alive, unlike the animal victims. Their bodies will be holy, as any sacrifice must be, set apart for God. They will be acceptable to God, in the way that the blood of bulls and goats could never be. This will be their 'spiritual worship' (*logikēn latreian*). Perhaps the translation of the adjective *logike* by the English word 'spiritual' is not accurate. This sacrifice will be a conscious one, not the offering of an irrational animal. The word is again used in I Peter 2.2 of milk, in contrast to physical milk. This offering by the Christian believers of their bodies as a living sacrifice will be non-physical; it will not involve mactation. It will also be conscious, an act of the will. St Paul deliberately used the word *thusia*, as if impressing upon his readers that the sacrifice of Christ on the Cross is now and henceforward to be offered by them in their offering of their own bodies. Christ's sacrifice continues in them. It is not the dropping of an outmoded concept or of a ritual act, but the continuation of that one act in and by the community of the faithful.

In Phil. 2.17, Paul says, 'Even if I am to be poured as a libation upon the sacrificial offering of your faith, I am glad . . . .' Paul's impending martyrdom is seen as a liquid offering, a libation, poured ritually over the *thusia kai leitourgia* which is their faith. The usage is metaphorical, but their faith in the sacrifice of Christ is the *main* sacrifice. His martyrdom is a libation poured on top of that sacrifice. The sacrifice will continue to be presented. Acts of martyrdom are to be seen, not as isolated acts of heroism but as blessings added to that ongoing sacrifice in the same way as libations of water were poured over animal sacrifice in the Temple. Peter says (I Peter 2.5) 'Come to him . . . be yourselves built into a spiritual house, to be a holy priesthood, to offer spiritual sacrifices acceptable to God through Jesus Christ.' The language is again that of the cultus, but applied to the work of the body of the faithful who will not immolate themselves literally, but will offer (*anenegkai*) spiritual sacrifices (*pneumatikas thusias*) as a holy priesthood. Again this is to be done through (*dia*) Christ. The sacrifice is presented to God by and in the body which is set apart for God. This prolonging of the sacrifice of Christ in the ongoing life of the body must underlie St Paul's remarks about himself in Col. 1.24, 'In my flesh I fill up what is lacking in Christ's afflictions, for the sake of his body, that is, the church.' As many a commentator has pointed out, this cannot mean that Paul saw Christ's death as in any way inadequate for the church, but his claim is that something has been left for him (Paul) to do by way of supplement.

This is to apply Jesus' sacrifice to the church of St Paul's day in the life of the body. In Paul's case he is talking about the application of the sacrifice to one member of the body, Paul himself. In no way does this threaten the uniqueness and 'once-for-all' nature of Christ's sacrifice. (It is indeed strange that many Protestant theologians are eager to accept that Paul's sacrificial language in this place does not undermine Christ's sacrifice, when Paul in no way apologizes for his language. Yet they refuse to accept assurances that the language of sacrifice applied to the Eucharist also does not undermine Christ's sacrifice.) Nothing could threaten the unique character of Christ's sacrifice in Paul's gospel. Nor does he mean that the saints (which, in the Corpus Paulinum, means the Christian people) or any one else, can add to the effectiveness of Christ's sacrifice. What Paul means is that the sacrifice of Christ has to be worked out in each generation of the Body's continuing life – and that can involve suffering-in-sacrifice to the extent of death.

Hebrews 13.15–16 says, 'Through him (Jesus) then let us continually offer up a sacrifice of praise to God, that is the fruit of lips that acknowledge his name. Do not neglect to do good and to share what you have, for such sacrifices are pleasing to God.' It might appear that animal sacrifices are to be replaced by the sacrifice of praising and doing good and sharing. But this has to be done through Jesus, who, in the language of the Epistle to the Hebrews, is our total sacrifice. We cannot repeat the unrepeatable, but we can apply it, continue it, remember it in the Hebrew sense of remembering, in the acts of the ongoing covenant community, in doing good and in sharing.

Jesus left two ways of applying his sacrifice to the continuing life of the church. He left a body which, though not practising immolation, would continue to give to God all that content of Christ's sacrifice that made it unique and all-embracing. As for Christ, as also for the continuation of his sacrifice, this will involve suffering in sacrifice – if Christ was the fulfilment of the servant then so is the church. If he suffered then the church will suffer. This body would continue to proclaim, through its cultus, the once-for-all completed sacrifice of its Lord. Thus a church without faith, or loving and caring community life, but nevertheless holding Eucharist, is a travesty of *Christ's* sacrifice and is merely presenting a dumb-show to itself. Also a church living out its gospel in terms of mission, evangelism and social concern is in danger of losing its roots in the sacrifice of Jesus and of producing

either a personal Jesus cult or good works, or both, in which it is hard
to see the real Jesus or Peter and Paul and John as proclaimed by their
writings. It would qualify for that acid gibe: 'The amazing thing about
the Jesus of the liberal Protestant is that anyone bothered to crucify
him.'

The claim and challenge of the New Testament is not that sacrifice
is ended but that sacrifices are ended and fulfilled in the one and only
sacrifice offered once and for all. All the elements of uniqueness are
there. Two opposite problems arise for the Christian religion: (A)
There are Christians belonging to cultures where sacrifices are still
offered. In some instances Christians belonging to those cultures have
been encouraged to continue sacrificing while at the same time
claiming the benefits of Christ's sacrifice. In many African cultures
this is the case. The sacrifice of Jesus Christ is proclaimed in the
Eucharist Sunday by Sunday and salvation in the name of Jesus
genuinely accepted: yet also animals are sacrificed in respect for the
ancestors and there are many teachers who would encourage these two
aspects of cultus to continue side by side. They would see no
contradiction between the uniqueness of Christ's sacrifice and the
multitude of sacrifices offered to or with the ancestors. Now many
motives are involved in this. But it would help to draw a distinction
between sacrifices that reconcile or obtain benefits or avert harm and
those that celebrate relationship, between sacrifices of atonement and
impetrative sacrifices on the one hand and thanksgiving and community-building sacrifices on the other. It would also help if clear
ideas of the meaning and functions of ancestors were defined.
Ancestors are not ancient atavistic spirits or ghosts haunting ancient
tombs, but bearers of the continuing life of the community, like the
parents to whom respect is due under the terms of the fifth
commandment. There must also be no avoiding of issues by
circumlocutions. It is rather more than mere deference or 'respect'
that is paid to ancestors and if the third-century Christians had a
problem in being asked to give 'respect' to the emperor, so also there
must be some problem areas connected with the ancestors in present-
day Africa. Also the term 'service' is not an accurate translation of, for
example, *idini* (Xhosa), which certainly is more accurately translated
as 'sacrifice' and is used of what is offered to the ancestors. There is a
strong current within African Christianity that rejects all forms of
cultus connected with the ancestors. An African colleague used to tell
me that his family had accepted Christ and rejected the traditional

cultus without any reference to white missionaries. He would also say that whenever he heard that ancestral spirits had threatened disaster and demanded sacrifice, he then knew for certain that these were no true ancestors, who would never threaten disaster. They were demons and must be told to begone.

On the other hand, the ongoing life of the community does not only concern those who at any given moment are actually living at any given time. It should express solidarity with 'the cloud of witnesses', those who have been members of the body – the assumption expressed somewhat coldly in the theological expression, 'the communion of saints' (unless that phrase means 'communion in holy *things*'). It is also expressed rather more warmly in the invocation or deprecation of the saints in the Catholic tradition. Indeed many black theologians have pleaded eloquently for a consideration of the veneration or respect of the ancestors to be considered as a different mode of invocation of the saints. There are several problems involved here – not insuperable, but still real. First, in popular Catholic devotion, the invocation of the saints has been addressed, not to the vast multitude of the faithful departed, but to the spiritual thoroughbreds amongst them – 'the greats'. Although there have been tendencies for French Christian to invoke French saints (and a refusal on the part of such as Bishop Stradling to invoke those saints such as Joan of Arc who might be considered to be anti-English) and so on across the nations, the saints have never been limited to 'family' – they are not the departed 'godfathers'. Also, the saints either in the New Testament meaning of the whole church, or in the subsequent meaning of the 'specials', has always been limited to those who have accepted Christ, whereas no African theologians would be willing so to limit their ancestry. The third problem is the Protestant (particularly Reformed) blockage concerning the communion of the saints. Doubtless this has been provoked by chantry chapels, masses for the wealthy dead and what has seemed like the elevation of certain saints into the position of God-substitutes. But whatever the causes may be, there is no possibility of dialogue between traditional Western Protestantism and Africa about the ancestors, except by some unsatisfactory theology of coexistence. At the very least, however it must be recognized that the African (and other third-world), practice of sacrifice, linked to respect for the ancestors, has a tremendous potential for flagging Western faith and theology. It brings sacrifice right back in the forefront, where it belongs in the biblical tradition. It emphasizes the importance of the ongoing roles of the community in offering that one sacrifice in its continuing life, embracing living and departed; and it effectively fills in the chasm in Western theology between intellectual faith and earthy cultures. What still remains to be faced is the unique and exclusive nature of Jesus' sacrifice and the roles of faithful suffering sacrificing that this demands of his church. This leads us to restate the new meanings that cling to the Cross and distinguish that sacrifice from all others. It is this that will give content to the Eucharist and to the outworking of sacrifice in the body of the faithful. First Christ was both rational and utterly obedient to the Father when he was offered up. Gethsemane shows this. Utter submission and rational obedience to the declared will of God now is within the meaning of sacrifice. Secondly, Christ willingly offers all, including suffering and including his life, holding back nothing, to the Father and for the world. This is also the content of the continuing sacrifice of the body – all is offered to God and for the world. Thirdly, his sacrifice is an act of repentance and faith, which actually spreads around the scene at Calvary, in that one of the thieves on a nearby cross enters into repentance with him. Repenting and encouraging repentance is involved in the continuing sacrifice of the body.

Fourthly, the Cross demonstrates Christ's perfect freedom. He is bound by no influences either of this world or of Satan's world or of any other. He is free to offer, free to suffer, free to die. The Cross is an act of liberation and it is *that* liberation theology that is the proclamation of the body. The church is the association, *par excellence*, of free people, freed by Christ. It is therefore completely free to proclaim freedom and to bring about freedom, provided that freedom ensures freedom for all.

Fifthly, Christ's sacrifice is done in utter truth and utter love. This can be said of no other act of sacrifice ever offered or to be offered. Truth and love must dominate the life of the body. If it does not do so, then its sacrifice is not that of Christ. Christ is not then being truly presented in the eucharistic sacrifice or in any other way – it is being misrepresented and Christ himself is being misrepresented.

Lastly, Christ's sacrifice is claimed by the victim and by his followers to be, not for one person, or for one family or for one nation or race, or for one planet, but for the whole cosmos. This is brought out most clearly in the fourth gospel. As Dom Gregory Dix (1945: 744) pointed out in his rapturous discourse about the Eucharist, the eucharistic sacrifice applies to 'every conceivable human circumstance, for every conceivable human need'. If that is a description of the scope of the Eucharist, *a fortiori* it is the description of Christ's sacrifice. It is no hyperbole to say that, in true Christian teaching the sacrifice of Jesus Christ *is* the past, present and future of the universe, and that the Body of the faithful offers this sacrifice for the world by proclaiming it in worship and in life.

What Teilhard de Chardin saw was a vision of a world perfected in Christ and through his sacrifice. 'And since the time when Jesus was born, when He finished growing and died and rose again, *everything has continued to move because Christ has not yet completed His own forming.* He has not yet gathered in to Himself the last folds of the Garment of flesh and love which His disciples are making for Him. *The mystical Christ has not yet attained His full growth.* In the pursuance of this engendering is situated the ultimate spring of all created activity . . . Christ is the Fulfilment even of the natural evolution of beings' (1964: 305).

There is a Russian icon, whose subject is the sacrifice of Isaac; in it the *aqedah* is portrayed in a highly iconographic and allegorical way. Isaac is a mere child and is being presented from one old man to another by the ministry of a third. It is of course a representation of the Trinity. At the heart of the life of God is sacrifice. The Movement of the Holy Trinity is the perfection of all offering. At this point all religions meet, as the Indian sages believed – in sacrifice in which the movement of the cosmic and celestial order finds its perfect expression.

In the heart of God, sacrifice is the eternal offering of mutual love of the persons of the Holy Trinity. In the world the offering of sacrifice takes and has taken many forms. All these forms, we believe, find their final expression, foreshadowed in the *aqedah* and outlined in the servant, in the perfect sacrifice, racked with the suffering caused by the world's alienation from its Creator, of Jesus Christ, the anointed King. This the church sets forth and acts out in all its members upon and for the world, until it will finally be taken up into the sacrifice of the Trinity in mutual love.

BIBLIOGRAPHY

Aquinas, T. *Summa Theologica*, Blackfriars edition, 60 vols., Eyre and
    Spottiswoode London 1963–76
Ashby, G.W.E.C. *Theodoret of Cyrrhus as Exegete of the Old Testament*,
    Rhodes University Grahamstown 1972
Augustine *De Civitate Dei*, tr. H. Bettenson (Pelican Classics), Penguin
    Books London 1972
Aulen, G. *Christus Victor*, tr. A.G. Hebert, SPCK London 1931
—*Eucharist and Sacrifice*, tr. E.H. Wahlström, Oliver and Boyd Edinburgh
    1958
Barrosse, T. 'The Passover and the Paschal Meal', *Concilium* 10.4, London
    1968, 13–18
Barth, M. *Was Christ's Death a Sacrifice?* (*Scottish Journal of Theology*
    Occasional Papers 9), Edinburgh 1961
Bauer, J.B. 'Lamb of God' in J.B. Bauer, *Encyclopedia of Biblical Theology*
    vol. 2, Sheed and Ward London 1970, 478–9
Beattie, J. *Other Cultures*, Cohen and West London 1964
—'On Understanding Sacrifice' in *Sacrifice*, ed. M.F.C. Bourdillon,
    Academic Press London 1980, 29–44
Bernard, J.H. *The Gospel according to John* (International Critical Commen-
    tary), T. & T. Clark Edinburgh 1928
Bolle, K.W. 'A World of Sacrifice', *History of Religions* 23, Chicago 1982,
    37–63
Bonner, C. Editor, *The Homily on the Passion by Melito of Sardis, with some
    fragments of the Apocryphal Ezekiel* (Studies and Documents 12),
    University of Pennsylvania, Philadelphia and London 1940
Bourassa, F. 'Expiation', *Science et Esprit* 22, fasc. 2, Montreal 1970
Box, G.H. 'The Jewish Antecedents of the Eucharist', *Journal of Theological
    Studies* 3, Oxford 1902, 357–69
—'St Luke 22. 15–16', ibid. 10, 1909, 106–7
Briggs, C.A. and E.G. *The Book of Psalms* (International Critical Commen-
    tary), T. & T. Clark Edinburgh 1909
Brock-Utne, A. 'Eine religionsgeschichtliche Studie zu dem ursprungliche
    Passahopfer', *Archiv für Religionswissenschaft* 31, Leipzig 1934, 272–8
Brown, J.R. *Temple and Sacrifice in Rabbinic Judaism*, London 1938
Brunner, E. *The Mediator*, tr. O. Wyon, Lutterworth London 1934
Büchler, A. *Studies in Sin and Atonement in the Rabbinic Literature of the First
    Century* (Jewish College Publications 11), Oxford University Press 1928
Burkill, T.A. 'The Last Supper', *Numen* 3, Leiden 1956, 161–77
Burkitt, F.C. 'The Last Supper and the Paschal Meal', *Journal of Theological
    Studies* 17, Oxford 1916, 291–7
Cadoux, C.J. 'The Religious Value of Sacrifice', *Expository Times* 58,
    Edinburgh 1947, 43–6

Calvin, J. *Institutes of the Christian Religion*, ed. J.T. McNeill, tr. F.L. Battles (Library of Christian Classics 21), SCM Press London 1960

Cassirer, E. *Philosophie der symbolischen Formen* vol. 2, Darmstadt 1973

Cazelles, H. Review of L. Moraldi, *Espiazione Sacrificiale* (see below), *Vetus Testamentum* 8, Leiden 1958, 312–16

Chantraine, P. 'Les noms de l'agneau en Grec: *arēn* et *amnos*', *Corolla Linguistica, Festschrift Ferdinand Sommer*, Wiesbaden 1955, 12–19

Chrysostom, J. *Hom. in Coemet. et Cruc.*, *Opera omnia* 2, ed. B. de Montfaucon, 2nd ed., Gaume Paris 1838, 469–75 (cited by number and letter in central column, 397–402)

—*Prod. Judae*, ibid. 444–55 (376–85)

—*Hom. 1–34 in Hebr.*, ibid. 12, 1838, 1–452 (1–318)

Clooney, F.X. 'Sacrifice and its Spiritualization in the Christian and Hindu Traditions', *Harvard Theological Review* 78, 1985, 361–80

Cooke, B. 'Synoptic Presentation of the Eucharist as Covenant Sacrifice' *Theological Studies* 21, Baltimore 1960, 1–44

Couratin, A.H. 'The Sacrifice of Praise', *Theology* 58, No. 422, London 1955, 285–91

Cross, L.B. 'Sacrifice in the Old Testament' in *The Atonement in History and Life*, ed. L.W. Grensted, SPCK London 1929, 33–64

Curtiss, S.I. 'The Semitic Sacrifice of Reconciliation', *The Expositor* 6.6, London 1902, 454–62

Cyprian *Epistle 63*, Migne, *Patrologia Latina* 4, cols. 383–401

Cyril of Jerusalem *Mystagogical Catecheses* 5.8–10, Migne, *Patrologia Graeca* 33, col. 1065

Dahood, M. *Psalms* (Anchor Bible), Doubleday New York 1969

Daly, R.J. *The Origins of the Christian Doctrine of Sacrifice*, Darton, Longman and Todd London 1978

Davies, D.J. 'An Interpretation of Sacrifice in Leviticus', *Zeitschrift für die alttestamentliche Wissenschaft* 89, Berlin 1977, 387–99

Davies, W.D. *Paul and Rabbinic Judaism*, SPCK London 1948

de Boer, P.A.H. 'An Aspect of Sacrifice' in *Studies in the Religion of Ancient Israel* (Supplements to *Vetus Testamentum* 23), Leiden 1972, 27–47

de Cock, J. 'I Valore Religioso dei Sacrifici dell 'Antico Testamente', *Bibbia et Oriente* 2, Milan 1960, 6–10

de Guglielmo, A. 'Sacrifice in the Ugaritic Texts', *Catholic Biblical Quarterly* 17, Washington 1955, 76–96 (196–216)

de Heusch, L. *Sacrifice in Africa – a Structuralist Approach*, Manchester University Press 1985

Denney, J. *The Christian Doctrine of Reconciliation*, Hodder and Stoughton London 1917

Des Knaben Wunderhorn: Alte Deutsche Lieder, collected by L.A. von Arnim and C. Brentano, vol. 1, Heidelberg and Frankfurt 1906

de Vaux, R. *Ancient Israel: its Life and Institutions*, tr. J. McHugh, Darton, Longman and Todd London 1961

—*Studies in Old Testament Sacrifice*, University of Wales Press, Cardiff 1964

Devreesse, R. 'Le Christianisme dans la péninsula sinaïtique des origines à l'arrivée des Mussulmans', *Revue Biblique* 49, Paris 1940, 205–23

Dewar, L. 'The Biblical Use of the Term "Blood"', *Journal of Theological Studies*, n.s. 4, Oxford 1953, 204–8

Didascalia et Constitutiones Apostolorum, ed. F.X. Funk, Paderborn 1905

Dillistone, F.W. *Christianity and Symbolism*, Collins London 1955

Dix, Dom G. *The Shape of the Liturgy*, Dacre Press London 1945

Dobbie, R. 'Deuteronomy and the Prophetic Attitude to Sacrifice', *Scottish Journal of Theology* 12, Edinburgh 1959, 67–82

Dodd, C.H. '*Ilaskesthai*, its cognates, derivatives and synonyms in the Septuagint', *Journal of Theological Studies* 32, Oxford 1931, 352–60

—*The Epistle of Paul to the Romans* (Moffatt New Testament Commentary), Hodder and Stoughton London 1932

—*The Bible and the Greeks*, Hodder and Stoughton 1935

—*The Interpretation of the Fourth Gospel*, Cambridge University Press 1953

Douglas, M. *Purity and Danger*, Routledge and Kegan Paul London 1966

Downing, J. 'Jesus and Martyrdom', *Journal of Theological Studies*, n.s. 14, Oxford 1963, 279–93

Driver, G.R. 'Three Technical Terms in the Pentateuch', *Journal of Semitic Studies* 1, Manchester 1956, 97–105

du Plessis, P.J. 'The Lamb of God in the Fourth Gospel' in *A South African Perspective on the New Testament*, ed. J.H. Petzer and P.J. Hartin, Brill Leiden 1987, 136–47

Durkheim, E. *The Elementary Forms of the Religious Life*, tr. J.W. Swain, 3rd ed., Allen and Unwin London 1954

Eichrodt, W. *Theology of the Old Testament*, tr. J. Baker (Old Testament Library), 2 vols., SCM Press London 1961, 1967

Eissfeldt, O. *Molk als Opferbegriff im Punischen und Hebräischen und das Ende des Gottes Moloch*, Halle 1935

Evans-Pritchard, E.E. *Nuer Religion*, Clarendon Press Oxford 1956

—'The Meaning of Sacrifice among the Nuer' (Henry Myers Lecture), *Journal of the Royal Anthropological Institute of Great Britain and Ireland* 84, London 1954, 21–33

Farrer, A.M. 'The Eucharist in I Corinthians' in *Eucharistic Theology Then and Now* by R.E. Clements and others (Theological Collections 9), SPCK London 1968, 15–33

Février, J.G. 'Les rites sacrificiels chez les Hébreux et à Carthage', *Revue des Études Juives* 4.3. 123, Paris 1964, 7–18

Franks, R.S. *The Atonement*, Oxford University Press 1934

Frazer, J.G. *The Golden Bough*, 3rd ed., 12 vols., Macmillan London 1907–15

—*Totemism and Exogamy*, vol 4, Macmillan London 1910

Freud, S. *Totem and Taboo*, tr. J. Strachey (Complete Works vol. 13), Hogarth Press London 1955

Füglister, N. *Die Heilsbedeutung des Pascha* (Studien zum Alten und Neuen Testament 8), Munich 1963

Gärtner, B. *John 6 and the Jewish Passover* (Coniectanea Neotestamentica 17), Lund 1959

Girard, R. 'La violence et le vrai savoir de l'homme', *Corporation Canadienne des Sciences Religieuses* 10.1, 1981

Glasson, T.F. 'The "Passover", a Misnomer, the meaning of the Verb

Pasach', *Journal of Theological Studies*, n.s. 10, Oxford 1959, 79–84

Goody, J.R. *Death, Property and the Ancestors*, Tavistock Publications London 1962

Gray, G.B. *Sacrifice in the Old Testament: its Theory and Practice*, Clarendon Press Oxford 1925

Gray, J. *The Legacy of Canaan: the Ras Shamra Texts and their Relevance to the Old Testament* (Supplements to *Vetus Testamentum* 5), Leiden 1957

Green, M. 'Christ's Sacrifice and Ours' in *Guidelines: Anglican Evangelicals Face the Future*, ed. J.I. Packer, Falcon Books London 1967, 87–117

Gregory of Nazianzus *Epistle* 171, Migne, *Patrologia Graeca* 37, cols. 280–1

Guttmann, A. 'The End of the Jewish Sacrificial Cult', *Hebrew Union College Annual* 38, Cincinnati 1967, 137–48

Hall, S.G. 'The Origins of Easter' (paper delivered at the Seventh International Patristic Conference, Oxford 1975), *Studia Patristica* 15 (Texte und Untersuchungen 128), Berlin 1984, 554–67

Haran, M. 'The Passover Sacrifice' in *Studies in the Religion of Ancient Israel* (Supplements to *Vetus Testamentum* 23), Leiden 1972, 86–116

Harrison, J.E. *Prolegomena to the Study of Greek Religion*, 3rd ed., Cambridge University Press 1922

Hicks, F.C.N. *The Fullness of Sacrifice*, 3rd ed., Macmillan London 1946

Higgins, A.J.B. *The Lord's Supper in the New Testament* (Studies in Biblical Theology 6), SCM Press London 1952

Hillyer, N. 'The "Lamb" in the Apocalypse', *Evangelical Quarterly* 39, Exeter 1967, 228–36

Hippolytus *The Treatise on the Apostolic Tradition*, ed. G. Dix, SPCK London 1937

Hobley, C.W. *Bantu Beliefs and Magic*, 2nd ed., H.F. and G. Wetherby London 1938

Hooke, S.H. *The Siege Perilous: Essays in Biblical Anthropology and kindred subjects*, SCM Press London 1959

Hooker, M.D. *Jesus and the Servant*, SPCK London 1959

Hubert, H., and Mauss, M. *Sacrifice, its Nature and Function*, Cohen and West London 1964

Ingham, J.M. 'Human Sacrifice at Tenochtitlan', *Comparative Studies in Sociology and History* 2.1, 1984

James, E.O. *Sacrifice and Sacrament*, Thames and Hudson London 1962

Jeremias, J. *The Eucharistic Words of Jesus*, tr. N. Perrin (New Testament Library), SCM Press London 1966

Johnson, A.R. 'Aspects of the Use of the Term *Panim* in the Old Testament', *Festschrift Otto Eissfeldt*, Halle 1947, 155–9

Kapelrud, A.S. *The Ras Shamra Discoveries and the Old Testament*, tr. G.W. Anderson, Blackwell Oxford 1965

Kaufmann, Y. *The Religion of Israel*, tr. M. Greenberg, Allen and Unwin London 1961

Kennett, R.H. *Old Testament Essays*, Cambridge University Press 1928

Kidner, D. *Sacrifice in the Old Testament* (Tyndale Old Testament Lecture), Tyndale Press London 1952

—'Sacrifice – Metaphors and Meaning', *Tyndale Bulletin* 33, Cambridge 1982, 119–36
Kilian, R. *Isaaks Opferung* (Stuttgarter Bibelstudien 44), Stuttgart 1970
Kilpatrick, G.D. *The Eucharist in Bible and Liturgy*, Cambridge University Press 1983
Knox, J. *The Death of Christ*, Collins London 1959
Koehler, L. *Old Testament Theology*, tr. A.S. Todd, Lutterworth London 1957
Kraus, H.J. *Worship in Israel*, tr. G. Buswell, Blackwell Oxford 1966
Kroeber, A.L. 'Totem and Taboo: an Ethnological Psychoanalysis', *American Anthropologist*, n.s. 22, Washington 1920, 48ff.
Kruse, H. 'Die "dialektische Negation" als semitisches Idiom', *Vetus Testamentum* 4, Leiden 1955, 385–400
Kuhn, K.G. 'The Lord's Supper and the Communal Meal at Qumran' in *The Scrolls and the New Testament*, ed. Krister Stendahl, SCM Press London 1958, 65–93
Langdon, S. 'The History and Significance of Carthaginian Sacrifice', *Journal of Biblical Literature* 23, Norwood, Mass. 1904, 79–93
Lattey, C. 'The Prophets and Sacrifice: a Study in Biblical Relativity', *Journal of Theological Studies* 42, Oxford 1941, 155–65
Leach, E. 'Ritual', *International Encyclopedia of Social Science*, New York 1968
—'The Logic of Sacrifice' (unpublished), 1975
Lévi, I. 'Le Sacrifice d'Isaac et la Mort de Jésus' in *The Sacrifice of Isaac*, ed. Yassif, Makor 1984
Lévi, S. *La Doctrine de Sacrifice dans les Brahmanas* (Bibliothéque de l'école des hautes études: section des sciences religieuses 73), Paris 1966
Lévi-Strausse, C. *Totemism*, tr. J. Needham, Penguin Books London 1969
Lietzmann, H. *Mass and Lord's Supper: a Study in the History of the Liturgy*, tr. D.H.G. Reeve, Brill Leiden 1979
Löhr, M. *Das Räucheropfer im Alten Testament* (Schriften der Königsberger Gesellschaft Jahrgang 4, Heft 4), Halle 1927
Lohse, B. *Das Passafest der Quartodecimaner* (Beiträge zur Förderung Christliche Theologie 2.54), Gütersloh 1953
Loisy, A. *Essai historique sur le sacrifice*, Paris 1920
Lupi, J. 'Liturgical Symbolism in the Baptismal Homilies of St John Chrysostom and Theodore of Mopsuestia' (paper delivered at the Seventh International Patristic Conference, Oxford 1975)
Lyonnet, S., and Sabourin, L. *Sin, Redemption and Sacrifice: a Biblical and Patristic Study* (Analecta Biblica 48), Rome 1970
Malinowski, B. 'Magic, Science and Religion' in *Science, Religion and Reality*, ed. J Needham, Sheldon Press London 1925, 19–84
Manson, W. *The Epistle to the Hebrews*, Hodder and Stoughton London 1953
Marien, M.E. 'Massacre et sacrifice humain: deux cas d'interprétation', *Symposium International sur les Religions Préhistoriques*, Valcamonica 1972
Mascall, E.L. *Corpus Christi*, Longmans Green London 1953
Masure, E. *The Sacrifice of the Mystical Body*, tr. A Thorold, Burns and Oates

London 1954

Mauss, M. see Hubert

Mayer, R. 'The Sacrifice after the Destruction of the Second Temple', *Fourth World Congress of Jewish Studies*, Jerusalem 1965

McCarthy, D.J. 'The Symbolism of Blood and Sacrifice', *Journal of Biblical Literature* 78, Philadelphia 1969, 166–76

McKenzie, J.L. *Second Isaiah* (Anchor Bible), Doubleday New York 1967

Médebielle, A. 'Expiation', *Dictionnaire de la Bible*, Supplément, vol. 3, Paris 1938, cols. 1–262

Money-Kyrle, R.E. *The Meaning of Sacrifice*, Institute of Psychoanalysis London 1930

Montefiore, C.G., and Loewe, H. *A Rabbinic Anthology*, Macmillan London 1938

Moraldi, L. *Espiazione Sacrificale e Riti Espiatori nell' Ambiente Biblico e nell' Antico Testamento* (Analecta Biblica 5), Rome 1956

Morgenstern, J. 'Two Prophecies of the Fourth Century BC and the Evolution of Yom Kippur', *Hebrew Union College Annual* 24, Cincinnati 1953, 1–74

Morris, L. 'The Biblical Use of the Term "Blood"', *Journal of Theological Studies*, n.s. 3, Oxford 1952, 216–27

—*The Apostolic Preaching of the Cross*, Tyndale Press London 1955

Mosothoane, E.K. 'Christology and Faith: a Study in Hebrews in relation to the *Sitz-im-Leben* and Purpose of the Epistle' (unpublished thesis, Birmingham 1974)

Moule, C.F.D. 'Sanctuary and Sacrifice in the Church of the New Testament', *Journal of Theological Studies*, n.s. 1, Oxford 1950, 29–41

—'The Sacrifice of the People of God' in *The Parish Communion Today*, ed. D.M. Paton, SPCK London 1962, 78–93

Mowinckel, S. 'Kultus' in *Die Religion im Geschichte und Genenwart*, 3rd ed., ed. K. Galling, vol. 4, Tübingen 1960, cols. 120–26

—*The Psalms in Israel's Worship* tr. D.R. ap–Thomas, 2 vols., Blackwell Oxford 1962

Mozley, J.K. *The Doctrine of the Atonement*, Duckworth London 1915

Neusner, J. *Aphrahat and Judaism*, Brill Leiden 1971

Nikiprowetsky, V. 'La spiritualisation des sacrifices et let culte sacrificiel au Temple de Jérusalem chez Philon d'Alexandrie', *Semitica* 17, Paris 1967, 97–116

Noth, M. *Leviticus: a Commentary*, tr. J.E. Anderson (Old Testament Library), SCM Press London 1965

Oesterley, W.O.E. *The Jewish Background of the Christian Liturgy*, Clarendon Press Oxford 1925

Origen *Commentarii in Rom.*, Migne, *Patrologia Graeca* 14, cols. 833–1291

Östborn, G. *Yahweh and Baal, Studies in the Book of Hosea and Related Documents* (Lunds Unversitets Arsskrift, NF 1, Band 51.6), 1956

Parrinder, E.G. *African Traditional Religion*, Hutchinson London 1954

Parrot, A. *The Temple of Jerusalem* (Studies in Biblical Archaeology 5), London 1957

Pedersen, J. *Israel, its Life and Culture*, Oxford University Press 1940

Petuchowski, J.B. 'Do this in Remembrance of Me (I Corinthians 11.24)', *Journal of Biblical Literature* 76, Philadelphia 1957, 293–8

Phillips, A. *Ancient Israel's Criminal Law*, Blackwell Oxford 1970

Powers, J.M. *Eucharistic Theology*, Burns and Oates London 1968

Price, S.R.F. 'Between Man and God: Sacrifice in the Roman Imperial Cult', *Journal of Roman Studies* 70, London 1980, 28–43

Quarello, E. 'Per una Chiaraficazione della Realta del Sacrificio', *Salesianum* 27.3, Rome 1965, 355–81

Rashdall, H. *The Idea of Atonement in Christian Theology*, Macmillan London 1919

Rendtorff, R. *Studien zur Geschichte des Opfers im Alten Israel* (Wissenschaftliche Monographien zum Alten und Neuen Testament 24), Neukirchen-Vluyn 1967

Reventlow, H. Graf *Problems of Old Testament Theology in the Twentieth Century*, Fortress Press Philadelphia 1985

Richardson, A. *An Introduction to the Theology of the New Testament*, SCM Press London 1958

Rivière, J. *The Doctrine of the Atonement*, tr. L. Cappadelta, International Catholic Library London 1909

Robertson Smith, W. *Lectures on the Religion of the Semites: The Fundamental Institutions*, A. and C. Black Edinburgh 1909

—*The Old Testament in the Jewish Church*, 2nd ed., A. and C. Black London and Edinburgh 1892

Rowley, H.H. *From Moses to Qumran: Studies in the Old Testament*, Lutterworth London 1963

Sabourin, L. *Priesthood: a Comparative Study* (Studies in the History of Religion 25: Supplements to *Numen*), Leiden 1973

— see also under Lyonnet

Saydon, P.P. 'Sin Offering and Trespass Offering', *Catholic Biblical Quarterly* 8, Washington 1946

Schmid, R. *Das Bundesopfer in Israel: Wesen, Ursprung und Bedeutung der Alten Testamenten Schellamim* (Studien zum Alten und Neuen Testament, Band 9), Munich 1964

Segal, J.B. *The Hebrew Passover from the Earliest Times to AD 70* (London Oriental Series 12), Oxford University Press 1963

Skinner, J. *Prophecy and Religion*, Cambridge University Press 1922

Smart, J.D. *History and Theology in Second Isaiah*, Westminster Press Philadelphia 1965

Snaith, N. 'The Sin-offering and the Guilt-offering', *Vetus Testamentum* 15, Leiden 1965, 73–80

—*Leviticus and Numbers* (Century Bible), London 1967

Soggin, J.A. 'A Proposito di Sacrifici di Fanciulli e di Culto dei Morti nell' Antico Testamento', *Oriens Antiquus* 8, Rome 1969, 215–17

Speiser, E.A. *Genesis* (Anchor Bible), Doubleday New York 1960

Spicq, C. *L'Épître aux Hébreux*, Paris 1953

Spiegel, S. *The Last Trial: on the Legends and Lore of the Command to Abraham to Offer Isaac as a Sacrifice: The Akedah*, tr. J. Goldin, Schocken Books New York 1967

Stibbs, A.M. *The Meaning of the Word 'Blood' in Scripture* (Tyndale New Testament Lecture), Tyndale Press London 1948
—*Sacrament, Sacrifice and Eucharist*, Tyndale Press London 1961
Strobel, A. 'Der Passa-Erwartung als urchristliches Problem in Lc 17.20f.', *Zeitschrift für die neutestamentliche Wissenschaft und die Kunde der älteren Kirche* 49, Berlin 1958, 157–96
Taylor, V. *Jesus and his Sacrifice: a Study of the Passion Sayings in the Gospels*, Macmillan London 1937
Teilhard de Chardin, P. *The Future of Man*, tr. N. Denny, Collins London 1964
Theodoret of Cyrrhus *Thérapeutique des maladies helleniques*, tr. P. Canivet (Sources Chrétiennes 57), Paris 1958
Thompson, R.J. *Penitence and Sacrifice in Early Israel outside the Levitical Law*, Brill Leiden 1963
Trumbull, H.C. *The Blood Covenant, a Primitive Rite, and its Bearings on Scripture*, Scribners New York 1885
Turner, V. 'Sacrifice as Quintessential Process: Prophylaxis or Abandonment?', *History of Religions* 16, Chicago 1977, 189–215
van Baal, J. 'Offer, Sacrifice and Gift', *Congress of the International Association for the History of Religions*, Lancaster 1975
van der Leeuw, G. *Religion in Essence and Manifestation*, Allen and Unwin London 1938
van Gennep, A. *The Rites of Passage*, tr. M.B. Vizedom and G.L. Caffee, Routledge and Kegan Paul London 1960
van Imschoot, P. *Theology of the Old Testament*, tr. K. Sullivan and F. Buck, Desclee New York 1965
van Seters, J. *Abraham in History and Tradition*, Yale University Press, Newhaven 1975
van Unnik, W.C. '"Worthy is the Lamb", the Background of Apocalypse 5',*Mélanges bibliques en hommage au R.P. Béda Rigaux*, Gembloux 1970, 445–61
Vermes, G. *Scripture and Tradition in Judaism* (Haggadic Studies), Brill Leiden 1961
—'Redemption and Genesis 22' in *The Sacrifice of Isaac*, ed. Yassif, Makor 1984
Vinnicombe, P. 'The Ritual Significance of Eland (*taurotragus oryx*) Art in Southern Africa', *Symposium International sur les Religions Préhistoriques*, Valcamonica 1972
von Rad, G. *Genesis*, tr. J.H. Marks (Old Testament Library), SCM Press London 1961
—*Old Testament Theology* vol. 1, tr. D.M.G. Stalker, Oliver and Boyd Edinburgh 1962
Weiser, A. *The Psalms*, tr. H. Hartwell (Old Testament Library), SCM Press London 1962
Welch, A.C. *Prophet and Priest in Old Israel*, Blackwell Oxford 1953
Wellhausen, J. *Prolegomena to the History of Israel*, tr. J.S. Black and A. Menzies, A. and C. Black Edinburgh 1885
Wenham, G.J. *The Book of Leviticus* (New International Commentary on the

Old Testament), Eerdmans Grand Rapids 1979

Westcott, B.F. *The Epistle to the Hebrews*, Macmillan London 1889

Wheeler Robinson, H. *Inspiration and Revelation in the Old Testament*, Oxford University Press 1946

Whybray, R.N. *Thanksgiving for a Liberated Prophet: An Interpretation of Isaiah 53 (Journal of the Society for Old Testament Studies*, Supplement 4), Sheffield 1978

Widengren, G. *Religionsphänomenologie*, Berlin 1969

Wiles, M.F. 'The Theological Legacy of St Cyprian', *Journal of Ecclesiastical History* 14, London 1963, 139–49

Wright, G.E., and Fuller, R.H. *The Book of the Acts of God: Contemporary Scholarship Interprets the Bible*, Doubleday New York 1960

Würthwein, E. 'Kultpolemich oder Kultbescheid in Tradition und Situation', *Studien zur alttestamentlichen Prophetie, Festschrift Artur Weiser*, Göttingen 1963

Wyatt, H. 'Ugaritic Theology of Atonement', *Congress of the International Association for the History of Religions*, Lancaster 1975

Yerkes, R.K. *Sacrifice in Greek and Roman Religion and in Early Judaism*, A. and C. Black London 1953

Young, F. 'The Use of Sacrificial Ideas in Greek Christian Writers from the New Testament to John Chrysostom' (unpublished thesis, Cambridge 1967)

INDEX OF NAMES

Aaron, 65
Abel, 42
Abraham, 22, 42, 43, 63, 77, 89, 90, 123
Agag, 42
Aphraates, 98
Aqedah, The, 42, 77, 89, 123, 135
Aristotle, 83
Ashby, G. W., 87, 90
Athanasius, 57, 67
Augustine, 55, 90, 121
Aulen, G., 66, 99
Azazel, 34, 35, 66

Barnabas, Epistle of, 67, 90
Barrosse, T., 77
Barth, M., 42, 43, 46, 47, 58, 68, 76
Beattie, J., 8, 19
Bede, Venerable, 90
Bernard of Clairvaux, 120
Bernard, J. H., 85
Bertholet, A., 41
Bonner, C., 98
Bourassa, F., 33, 65
Box, G. H., 78
Briggs, C. A. & E. G., 46
Brock-Utne, A., 73
Brown, J. R., 51, 90
Brunner, E., 7, 79
Büchler, A., 50
Burkill, T. A., 79
Burkitt, F. C., 78

Cain, 42
Calvin, J., 31, 59, 67, 119
Cassirer, E., 17
Cazelles, H., 33

Chantraine, P., 88
Clement of Alexandria, 54
Clooney, F. X., 66
Cooke, B., 80, 95, 103, 115
Couratin, A. H., 103
Cross, L. B., 40
Curtiss, S. I., 95
Cyprian, 117
Cyril of Jerusalem, 115, 116
Cyrus, 124, 127

Dahood, M., 46
Daly, R. J., 40
David, 39
Davies, D. J., 38
Davies, W. D., 95
de Cock, J., 43
de Guglielmo, A., 40
de Heusch, L., 19
de Lugo, J., 118, 119
de Vaux, R., 15, 31, 32, 33, 38, 39, 70, 76, 83, 100, 101, 125
Denny, J., 67
Devreesse, R., 37
Dewar, L., 39
Didache, 107
Dillistone, F. W., 74
Diognetus, Epistle to, 54
Dix, G., 113, 114, 134, 135
Dodd, C. H., 66, 67, 83, 85, 87, 88
Douglas, M., 3, 7
Downing, J., 62
Driver, G. R., 35, 76
Du Plessis, P. J., 85
Duns Scotus, 58
Durkheim, E., 5, 14, 15, 16, 17

Eichrodt, W., 30, 32
Eissfeldt, O., 43
Elijah, 77
Eliot, T. S., 96
Ephrem, 90
Etheria, 112
Evans-Pritchard, E. E., 8, 10, 23
Ezekiel, 27, 31, 44, 46, 51
Ezra, 31

Falashas, The, 77
Farrer, A. M., 95
Frazer, J. G., 3, 12, 13
Freud, S., 9, 12
Füglister, N., 73, 74, 89, 95

Gärtner, B., 96
Girard, R., 18
Glasson, T. F., 69
Goody, J. R., 8, 27
Gray, G. B., 15, 34, 39, 44, 64, 70, 72, 76, 84
Green, M., 39
Gregory of Nazianzus, 116
Guttmann, A., 51

Hall, S. G., 98
Haran, M., 70
Harrison, J. E., 12
Heracleitus, 53
Hicks, F. C. N., 1, 81
Hiel, 42
Higgins, A. J. B., 88, 89, 103
Hillyer, N., 86
Hippolytus, 107, 115
Hooke, S., 110
Hooker, M., 61, 88, 96
Hubert, H. & Mauss, M., 10, 14, 20, 31

Ignatius of Antioch, 106
Ingham, J. M., 21
Irenaeus, 90, 107
Isaac, 42, 62, 77, 89, 90, 123, 135
Ishmael, Rabbi, 90
Isidore of Seville, 90

Jacob, 89

James, E. O., 58
Jastrow, M., 6
Jephthah, 42
Jeremiah, 127
Jeremias, J., 76, 77, 79, 82, 95, 104, 105, 106, 110
Johanan Ben Zakkai, 51
John the Baptist, 83, 84, 88, 90
John Chrysostom, 113, 116
John of Damascus, 97
Johnson, A. R., 30
Joseph, 77
Josiah, 39, 70, 73, 75
Justin Martyr, 51, 54, 67, 97, 107

Kapelrud, A. S., 27, 35
Kaufmann, Y., 27, 30, 32, 71
Kennett, R. H., 35
Kidner, D., 36, 39, 47
Kilian, R., 42
Kilpatrick, G. D., 106, 107
Knox, J., 100
Koehler, L., 3, 43
Kraus, H.-J., 38
Kroeber, A. L., 37
Kruse, H., 71
Kuhn, K. G., 109, 110

Laban, 89
Langdon, S., 27
Lattey, C., 45
Lazarus, 91, 92
Leach, E., 18, 23, 35, 41
Lévi, I., 89
Lévi, S., 16, 23, 24
Lévi-Strauss, C., 14
Lietzmann, H., 107
Loehr, M., 31
Löhse, B., 98
Loisy, A., 20, 24
Lupi, J., 110
Luther, M., 58
Lyonnet, S., see Sabourin

McCarthy, D. J., 37, 40, 74
McKenzie, J. L., 127, 128
Mahler, G., 84
Makkay, 21

Malinowski, B., 15
Manson, W., 63, 65
Mascall, E., 118
Masure, E., 118, 119
Mauss, M., see Hubert
Mayer, R., 51
Médebielle, A., 62, 89
Melchizedek, 66
Melito of Sardis, 96, 98, 111
Milgrom, 33
Money-Kyrle, E. R., 89
Montefiore, C. G., 52
Moraldi, L., 32, 41, 43
Morgenstern, J., 36
Morris, L., 39, 67
Moses, 27, 37, 39, 46, 64, 65, 74, 77, 127
Mosothoane, E. K., 64
Moule, C. F. D., 54, 67
Mowinckel, S., 23, 125
Mozley, J. K., 60

Narsai, 106
Nehemiah, 31
Neusner, J., 98
Nikiprowetsky, V., 53
Noah, 33
Noth, M., 41

Oesterley, W. O. E., 79
Origen, 68
Ostbornm, G., 28

Parrinder, G., 21
Parrot, A., 27
Paul, 11, 30, 54, 56, 57, 58, 59, 61, 63, 94, 95, 109
Pedersen, J., 71
Pelagius, 59
Petuchowski, J. B., 95
Philip, 123
Phillips, A., 34
Philo, 53, 77
Plato, 53, 83
Pliny, 110
Porphyry, 5
Powers, J. M., 106
Price, S. R. F., 24

Quarello, E., 28

Rabanus Maurus, 90
Radmilli, 21
Rashdall, H., 56, 58, 62
Rendtorff, R., 28, 29, 74
Reventlow, H. Graf, 42
Richardson, A., 90
Rivière, J., 60, 68
Robertson Smith, W., 12, 13, 17, 44
Rowley, H. H., 26, 32, 45, 71, 110
Rublev, A., 90

Sabourin, L., 34, 40, 56, 64, 65, 90
Sarah, 123
Saydon, P. P., 58
Schmid, R., 38
Segal, J. B., 35, 36, 69, 70, 71, 72, 74
Sellers, R. V. S., 56
Selwyn, E. G., 96
Skinner, J., 44
Smart, J. D., 127
Snaith, N., 33, 35
Soggin, J. A., 43
Speiser, E. A., 42
Spicq, C., 65, 91
Spiegel, S., 77
Stibbs, A. M., 39
Strobel, A., 91

Taylor, V., 44, 50, 61, 62, 91, 106, 113, 122
Teilhard de Chardin, P., 135
Tertullian, 90
Theodore of Mopsuestia, 113, 114, 115, 116
Theodoret of Cyrrhus, 55, 67, 90
Thomas Aquinas, 76, 112, 117
Thompson, R. J., 31, 111
Trumbull, H. C., 74

van Baal, J., 14
van der Leeuw, G., 15, 16, 23, 121, 122
van Gennep, A., 18
van Imschoot, P., 40
van Seters, J., 42, 43

van Unnik, W. C., 87
Vermes, G., 77, 89, 90
Vinnicombe, P., 10
von Rad, G., 36, 42, 47, 73

Welch, A. C., 73
Weiser, A., 43
Wellhausen, J., 17, 31, 70
Wenham, G. J., 28, 29, 32, 38, 62
Westcott, B. F., 37, 67

Wheeler Robinson, H., 46
Whybray, R. N., 123
Widengren, G., 106
Wright, G. E., 42
Würthwein, E., 46
Wyatt, H., 35

Yassif, E., 89
Yerkes, R. K., 6, 31, 44, 47
Young, F., 47, 53, 54, 55, 57, 67, 68, 73, 98

INDEX OF BIBLICAL REFERENCES

Genesis
4   29, 42
8.21   30
22   42, 43, 62, 89, 90

Exodus
5.1   70
12   69–77, 88, 90
15.1–8   74
24.4–8   39, 40
25.9, 40   66
29   29
34.25   72

Leviticus   13, 28, 38
1   29, 31, 62
4–5   32
8–10   35
15   40
17.11   40
17–26   96

Numbers   71
8.4   66
9.7, 13   72
28–29   29, 96

Deuteronomy   71
16   72, 73
21   40

I Samuel
13.12   30

II Samuel
24.15–25   36

I Kings
16.34   42
18.26   69

II Kings
16.13   29
23.21–23   73, 74

II Chronicles
30.2–27   75
35.1–18   35

Psalms
22   128
40.6   43
50.13   43
51.16f.   43, 46
72.1   125, 127

Isaiah
1.10–17   43
31.5   69
34.11   69
40–55   123–8
42.1–4   62, 127
49   124, 127
50   127
53   33, 61–3, 84f., 88–90, 96, 99, 124, 128
55.3   125

Jeremiah
7.21f.   43, 46, 71
11.19   84
31.8   77

Daniel   87

Hosea
6.6   43

Amos
4.4   43, 46
5.21–26   43, 46, 71

Micah   15
6.6–8   43, 45

Zechariah   87
5.5–11   35

Malachi
1.1   107
1.9   30

Matthew   78, 79
2.17   90
3.17   62
5.23f.   50
7.9–13   50
26.1   78
26.16–19   79
26.30   81
27.15   81

Mark   78
1.11   90
14.1f.   81
14.12–16   79, 82
14.22–25   93
14.26   81
15.6   81

Luke		*Romans*		*II Timothy*	
3.22	78, 81	3.21–26	52, 61, 66	4.6	62
22.1f.	81	4.1	68		
22.7–16	78, 79, 82, 90	12.1	54, 129	*Hebrews*	63–8, 97
				2.17	66
John	62, 78, 79, 80,	*I Corinthians*		9	95
	82, 85	5.6–8	78, 97, 103	13.15f.	131
1.19	90	11.23–26	94, 103	13.20	65, 95
1.29	83, 87, 88	15.20	103		
1.36	83, 88			*I Peter*	
3.16	90	*II Corinthians*		1.19	86, 88, 96
6	96	3.6	95	2.2	130
11.44f.	92			2.5	54, 130
11.5–57	81	*Galatians*			
12.1f.	91	4.24	95	*I John*	
12.12, 20	92			2.2	66
13.1	78	*Ephesians*			
18.28	92	2.13–17	95		
18.39	81			*Revelation*	86–8, 99,
19.32–37	93	*Philippians*			118
21	96	2.17	130	5.6	87
				7.14	87
Acts		*Colossians*		8.1–3	54, 58
8	88, 123	1.24	63, 130	11.19	54

Apocrypha and Pseudepigrapha

Ecclesiasticus		*Enoch*		*Testament of Joseph*	86
7.31	50	8.1	35		
35.1–7	52			*Testament of Levi*	51
50.11–15	50	*Jubilees*			
		18.18f.	77	*IV Maccabees*	
II Maccabees		49	73	6.27–29	62
7.37f.	62				
Wisdom		*Testament of Benjamin*			
18.6–9	75	3.8	85		

Rabbinica

Targum Neofiti	89	*Mishnah Yoma*	
		8	50